To my son, Landon

My hero, my best friend, my rock, and my greatest blessing.

Thank you for being unapologetically yourself, for making me

laugh every day, and for inspiring me to be a better person.

You are the best part of my life.

I love you, with my whole heart, forever.

# TEEN MOM SYNDROME

KAYLA CARLILE

# Contents

## INTRODUCTION

No matter who you are or where you are from, odds are, somebody you know is a teen mom. According to the Center for Disease Control and Prevention, a total of 194,377 babies were born to teen moms in 2017. I remember early in my pregnancy, people reassured me with stories about their neighbors, their aunts, their nieces, and their sisters who had been teenage mothers. I had no idea how many young moms had preceded me because our society doesn't amplify these voices or illuminate these stories.

When I use the term 'teen mom', I use it as an indefinite title. Even if your teenage years are far behind you, I believe that the experience of being a teen mom is something that you will embody and carry with you for the duration of your life. It affects who you are to your core- your personality, your idea of family, your access to education, your relationship with your parents, how you form friendships, how you date, who you are in relationships, how you parent, and more.

Over the years, I have often felt overwhelmed by emotions that I could not decipher, let alone explain to anybody else. It took time to come to the realization that there really is only a small margin of people who can understand the lens through which I am living, and they are other teen moms. I'm not saying that teen dads do not also have their own unique experience- I simply cannot write about it because I have not experienced it. So, I am here to write about my experience as a teen mom (although I am no longer a teenager) and a phenomenon I have grown to describe as 'teen mom syndrome'. If nothing else, at least this book will serve as a journal for me, a therapeutic outlet to think out loud and attempt to decipher my own identity.

I think it is important to acknowledge that teen moms in Western culture have a terrible reputation. Whether it be from MTV shows like Teen Mom and Sixteen and Pregnant, stereotypes, or actual experiences people have had with young mothers, I think it is safe to say that the phrase 'teen mom' does not hold a positive connotation. From a religious standpoint, teen moms are an easy target of judgement. Unlike most, their sins are advertised. There is no way to hide the fact that you had sex before marriage if you are visibly pregnant, unless you are the virgin Mary, but that's for a different book.

If you think you do not stereotype teen moms, I am here to tell you that you are (most likely) wrong. Heck, even I stereotyped teen moms before becoming one. Seeing a sixteen-year-old at the mall with a pregnant belly was something my eyes couldn't help but fixate on; I couldn't help but make negative assumptions about her life, her intelligence, her education, her future or lack thereof. I would look at her and think in my head, "that could never be me. I would never be that irresponsible, I would never be that stupid, I would never be that trashy." Oh, how my world quickly changed.

I am not here to say that the stereotypes about teen moms aren't true- actually, I would argue that some of them do hold some truth. According to the dictionary, a Stereotype is defined as *a widely held but fixed and oversimplified image or idea of a particular type of person or thing.* Instead of arguing against many of the stereotypes about teen mothers, I want to provide an inside perspective as to why they may behave in a way that the rest of society can't understand. Some examples of stereotypes about teen moms include: "They're irresponsible", "They don't know how to parent", "They're children having children", "All they do is party", "They're whores", "They sleep around", "Their parents raise their kids for them", "They're stupid", "They regret having their kids", "They end up on welfare", "They're doomed to fail", "Teen moms drop out of high school", or my favorite, which I heard a student whisper behind me as I squeezed my pregnant belly into my 10th grade biology desk, "I don't know why pregnant girls even come to school. Their lives are already over."

## MY BACKGROUND

I found myself pregnant at the age of fifteen. I will spare you the details because I am not here to write about my failed teenage romantic endeavors or engage in a religious debate about my moral compass, but I entered my first serious relationship as a freshman in high school and left the relationship as a pregnant sophomore. You can figure out what happened in between. Perhaps the result of us being two children (truly, we were just kids at the ages of 14/15) navigating their first serious romantic relationship, the relationship became unhealthy, and so it ended.

My hope in describing my experience is not to negate or invalidate that of any of the other people involved in my journey. After all, there are always two sides to every story. Each person mentioned in this book has their own story to tell, in which my character might be portrayed differently than the way I write about myself. I will be writing honestly about events as I remember them impacting me- although it is important to acknowledge that INTENT does not always equal IMPACT. Every individual has their own perspective that is *equally* valid.

Before I begin, I will preface by stating that I was incredibly fortunate to grow up in a home with two parents who loved me very much. I am thankful for my family and the childhood I had.

I grew up in a lower middleclass family in Springfield, Oregon. For most of my childhood, my mother was a stay at home mom and my father worked until evening every night at the county jail. By the time his key would turn in the front doorknob, I would be excitedly galloping down the hall to greet him. His eyes were always baggy and his face was always defeated. I never realized as a child how exhausted he always was from work, nor how emotionally draining his job was. I just saw it as *'dad's home from work, so now we can play'*.

"Will you play with me?" I would ask, but most nights he was too tired. If he did play with me, he would lay on my bedroom floor and we would take turns shooting a plush basketball into the plastic hoop he had hung over my bedroom door. I would tell him stories about my adventurous days at school, but he mostly just replied *'mmhmm'*s and nodded. I don't think he heard much of what I told him.

My time with my dad was sparse, and perhaps that's why it was my favorite. On the weekends he would let me come with him to the local hardware store to get whatever he needed for whatever project he had convinced my mom he needed to do around the house. I loved it because he would always let me pick out a candy bar or soda, and he even let me ride in the front seat of his old blue Ford Escort because there was no passenger airbag. The smell of lumber soon became the essence of my father-daughter experience.

My mom played with me too, but it seemed like most of her attention was focused on my little brother. He was 4.5 years younger than me, and when I found out I was having a brother instead of a sister, my four-year-old self was furious. Despite this initial dismay, I ended up being the one who named him and grew quite fond of this mysterious baby that entered our family.

Around the time he started kindergarten, my brother's teachers recommended to my parents that he be tested for autism. For whatever reason, my parents never had him tested, but I was positive growing up that he was autistic. His doctor mentioned the possibility that he had Asperger's Syndrome- a condition on the autism spectrum that can cause someone to be socially unaware and have an all-absorbing interest in specific topics. Both of these were inarguably true- first, there was Bob the Builder. As a two-year-old, he watched an unhealthy amount of it, had a bedroom full of every Bob the Builder toy you could imagine, and among his first words were "Bob". Around the time he turned three, it became apparent that he was falling behind developmentally. He was still only speaking a handful of words and referring to almost everything as "Bob". This eventually required years of speech therapy, which I find ironic, because now he is always the smartest and most well-spoken man in any room. His vocabulary triumphs mine by a landslide, and I am constantly Googling the definitions of words he uses.

Next was his obsession with Thomas the Train. This 3-5-year long fascination controlled every aspect of his life. As he progressed through elementary, middle, and high school, his fascinations went through many phases: Phineas and Ferb, Legos, Star Wars, Transformers. I spent many years jealous of the amount of my parent's attention that he consumed, although with adolescence he became more socially aware and became, out of nowhere, a social butterfly. Today, we are very close. He even animated a whole season of his own Transformers episodes and has quite the YouTube following. Despite our friendship now, as kids we hardly interacted, leaving me feeling like an only child with only her imagination to entertain her.

I was a shy and quiet child until you really got to know me. I spent my free time inhaling the words off the pages of books, writing stories so vigorously that my hand would ache, or drawing for hours on end. My mother was extremely religious and my father wasn't.

Every Sunday she would dress my brother and I in our nicer clothes and take us to church, whether we wanted to go or not. We went to church every Sunday and every Wednesday, rain or shine. I didn't really mind church- after class, there was always a table of donuts or cookies in the big gathering room.

My father wouldn't go to church with us. He had Sundays off, but he always had a football game that he insisted he couldn't miss. He would also express his discomfort with sitting in pews surrounded by people pretending to be perfect- looking back, he had severe social anxiety. Inviting my friends over put him in a mode of panic. So did family events. In fact, he had anxiety about most things: about driving, about swimming, about riding a bike, about large social groups, about being followed home from the store by an old inmate of his, about the house being broken into, about me being kidnapped, about getting a cell phone because cell phones caused cancer, and about going to church. I understood why- his childhood was one that deprived him of learning how to swim, how to ride a bike, how to drive. He was a troublemaker and spent most of his time grounded to his bedroom. The way it's been told, he spent most of his youth paying for his mischief and excluded from the family. He missed out on most of the experiences that normal children have. After barely finishing high school he joined the army at the age of seventeen and didn't get his driver's license until his late twenties. Recognizing how big of a role anxiety plays in my father's life has helped me to recognize my own struggles with anxiety that I learned growing up.

As a child, it felt like every moment that both of my parents were home was spent fighting. They both had tempers, and occasionally a dish would get thrown across the room or my mom would storm out of the house and drive away, not returning for hours. I spent a lot of those fights comforting my brother or distracting him by playing with him in his room with the door closed. Distracting him from the conflict helped me to distract myself too.

My parents often pulled me into their fights and make me pick sides. Most of the time, I picked my dad's side, because it was less pleasant to have him angry at me. For years I took his side on various issues- I think eventually my mother grew to resent me for that. Honestly, I spent many years waiting for the day my parents would announce a divorce- but that day never came. I had already planned out what each of their separate houses would probably be like and which bedroom I would like better. It seemed like they were opposites in every way possible and most days it didn't even seem like they enjoyed each other's presence. They never showed affection and growing up with their turbulent relationship has probably affected my adult relationships. For example, I hate public displays of affection. I just didn't grow up around it.

It wasn't until I was in middle school, about to enter high school, that my father started coming to church with us. For months I had begged him to come- I didn't like that he didn't come with us. My dad was my favorite person and all I wanted was to have my whole family together, even if it was just one day a week for an hour. Once he began coming, he had befriended most of the congregation and had embedded himself in the church community within a year. He started volunteering, starting joining Men's Groups, went on a mission trip to Mexico, and making friends. With these newfound friends and religious beliefs, I felt like he transformed into a different person. I watched as he became happier, less angry, more patient, and more outgoing. It was like getting a whole new dad.

In addition to Christianity, one thing that was stressed during my childhood was academic success. Raised by Catholic parents, my mother went to 12 years of private Catholic school before attending a private Christian University. She had graduated from a four-year university with a teaching degree, but ended up hating teaching, so she never used it. My dad barely finished high school and enlisted in the army at the age of 17.

It was pushed on me from a very young age that I had to be successful because they 'weren't'. They talked about wanting me to have the life they didn't have. I quickly learned that this meant money. They wanted me to make more money than them. My dad often joked that, once I had become rich and successful, I could help them out financially. This put a lot of stress on my shoulders as a kid. I let go of my passion to become a writer or an artist and started daydreaming about prestigious careers like being a lawyer or a doctor. Mostly, I wanted to be rich, so that I could pay off my parent's house and they would never fight about money again. It felt like they wanted me to be perfect.

The pressure on my academics sometimes felt overwhelming. I wasn't particularly pretty, athletic, or outgoing, so being successful academically was the only way I saw that I could please them. I was desperate to make them proud of me, I desperately wanted the attention that I felt was only given to my brother. For this reason, also, I often acted out and got myself into trouble.

I didn't really realize how much we struggled financially until I was in middle school and my father got laid off from his job at the jail. My mother didn't work and suddenly the already stressful financial fights became daily. Evening after evening, yelling and arguing and crying and stressing about how they would pay the bills filled the house. They were suddenly stuck relying on unemployment and food stamps. I felt secondhand embarrassment as I listened to my dad talk about how embarrassing it was using his food stamp card at the grocery store. I even tried to help him come up with a clever way to make the Oregon Trail card look like some kind of debit or credit card, so he could use it discreetly in checkout lines.

Eventually, my dad found employment and my parents regained their foothold, right about the time I was getting ready to start high school. I was determined to prove my academic potential. I had big dreams, dreams of going to college, getting rich, and making my parents proud of me. I even made the cheerleading team with my best friends and spent nearly every summer day leading up to freshman year at cheer practice. By the time high school started, I had lost most of the

15

chubbiness caused by years of TV dinners and watching television. For the first time, I felt like I had the potential to be popular. I was a cheerleader, I was starting at a new school with kids from other middle schools, I had slimmed down, and puberty had begun to work its magic on my body.

My first year of high school was exciting and fun. I went to school, hung out with friends, went to cheerleading practice, and talked to lots of boys. I was hardly spending any time at home and I was finally making friends with some of the other girls on the cheer team. I found myself in a bit of a shock as I realized that my peers were really doing all of the things of the teenage movies: drinking, smoking, having sex, skipping class, and getting into trouble. My friends and I were fairly innocent. We took pride in not participating in the "rowdy" activities that some of our classmates did. We didn't drink, smoke, have sex, or party. (*Okay, we may have skipped a few classes, but that's it.*)

By the end of my freshman year, I had my first real boyfriend. My parents were uneasy about this and monitored me strictly. They used apps to read my texts and limited our visits to a few hours at a time. There was a strict open-door policy at my parents' house and there were many fights between my parents and I about the relationship. Time progressed, a LOT happened, and I soon found myself pregnant as a new sophomore. The relationship came to a turbulent end.

I didn't talk to my parents about sex. My mother grew up Catholic- she went to 12 years of private Catholic school, and my dad was her first kiss. Sex before marriage was a sin in our household- or at least that was assumed to be the standard, because it was never really discussed. The one time I had asked my mom about sex was when I was in about the fifth grade. I had been reading my Bible in my room and stumbled across the word. With no idea what it was, I asked her. She went to her room and retrieved an illustrated children's book, a cartoon Christian rendition of the birds and the bees talk. Sex was something two *married* adults did to make a baby. The sperm found the egg and *wa-la*, baby. That was the extent of our sex discussion.

I didn't talk to my parents about boys at all. My personal life was very much kept separate from my family life. I learned early on that if I wanted to listen to the music my friends listened to, I had to do it in secret. If I wanted to have a boyfriend, I had to do it in secret. If I wanted to have a Myspace, I had to make it in secret. When I did want to do all of these things, I relied on my friends to teach me, because I surely wasn't going to get any help from my parents. My friends taught me how to dress, how to do my makeup, how to use a tampon, how to be 'cool'.

As I journeyed through my teenage years, I felt the usual teenage angst and dislike for my parents. They were too strict, too religious, they weren't cool, they had too many rules, and they just *didn't understand anything.* The relationship most strained by my adolescence was the one between my mother and I. In addition to having very little in common, we now had even *less* in common as my interests became makeup, fashion, boys, celebrities, my cell phone, music, and the internet. As I remember believing as a teenager, she lived in a fantasy Bible world and she would never understand me. Finding out her unwed teenage daughter was pregnant in high school only added to the divide between us.

My mother's favorite pastimes were doing puzzles and playing board games. After being a stay at home mom for most of my early childhood until my little brother was self-sufficient, she had found her nook in caregiving for the elderly and mentally handicapped. Raised by parents greatly affected by the Great Depression, she had grown up in a small house with five siblings. My grandparents lived extremely frugally- to put it nicely, their house was falling apart. During my childhood visits, I never really noticed the condition of their house. It wasn't until I got older that I realized how run down it truly was. So run down in fact, that upon both of their passing, the house was demolished. My grandmother passed away when I was in the fifth grade and I was devastated. My grandfather said he was ready to go right then, he had no desire to continue life without her. Yet, he lived another 10 years.

At Christmas and his birthday, my grandpa refused gifts. His socks had holes in them and his thrift store clothing never quite fit him right. His signature look was a matching tan shirt and pants- the kind a mechanic would wear, but he had never been a mechanic. He lived a modest life in his small, falling apart house. He loved his children and his grandchildren with all of his heart, and above all else, he loved God. He began a long journey with Alzheimer's, and even when he could no longer remember who I was, he could remember to attend Mass at church every day. At his funeral, the priest even spoke about how he would often show up before the sun was up, knocking on the priest's door and asking why the church was still locked. The priest would kindly let him know that he was 4 hours early and send him back home to bed. Even when he had been stripped of everything- his memory, his identity, and his livelihood, his devotion to God remained.

My mother took after her father in almost every way. She is frugal, religious, and humble. She went to college and focused on academics. She told me that she

tried alcohol only a few times in college and hated it-
she never drank again. She didn't watch television or
listen to music. Her life was devoted to prayer, religion,
her kids, and later in life, work. After college she moved
back home with her parents and worked at Bi-Mart,
until she met my father.

Her youth drastically contrasted my fathers. He
had joined the army at the age of 17 and spent 9 years
being carefree, partying, drinking, and being reckless.
To this day I'm not sure what they saw in each other,
but somehow, they are still together. My mother had a
friend whose husband knew my dad. The couple set up
a blind date game night. Beforehand, my dad's friend
told him to go "scout her out" at work. The story is that
he approached her at Bi-Mart and asked her where the
mud flaps were. She had no idea who he was, but
apparently my dad liked what he saw, because they went
on their blind date and ended up getting married in less
than a year, despite their contrasting personalities. Their
drastically different personalities directly impacted how
they each viewed my teenage pregnancy.

## PREGNANT

When I first discovered I was pregnant at fifteen, I was absolutely terrified to tell my parents. I prayed and prayed to God that it was a mistake. I prayed that I would wake up the next day and it would all be a dream. I promised God that, if he could make me not pregnant, I would never have sex before marriage again. I only lasted about a week before I ended up telling my parents, but that week of secrecy was torture.

When I had first suspected that I might be pregnant, I told my boyfriend and he told his sister. She came and picked me up from school after lunch. I skipped my afternoon class, which was unlike me, but on this particular day I had more pertinent concerns than a call home about skipping class. I climbed into her car shyly, putting my backpack between my knees. As I climbed in, I caught a glimpse of her backseat; a car seat, cluttered toys, a sippy cup tipped sideways, cracker crumbs spewed everywhere. *That might be my future.*

She drove me to Walgreens and bought me a pregnancy test while I waited nervously in the car. The day had started out brisk and had quickly gotten warmer, the way that fall mornings do. I could feel beads of sweat dripping from my armpits under my thick hoodie, but was too paralyzed by anxiety to take it off. Once she returned, she drove us to her parent's house. She assured me nobody would be home, and I prayed this was true. When we arrived and confirmed that the house was empty, she sent me in the bathroom with the test and instructions.

After struggling to pee on that scary plastic stick, I snapped the cap back on, set it on the counter, and hastily scurried down the hallway to the living room. We made small talk as we waited for her phone timer to signal that three minutes had passed. I let my eyes wander across the room, trying to notice things that would take my attention away from the seconds that were creeping by more slowly than time had ever moved before. I rubbed my thumb against the microfiber of the couch, back and forth, back and forth, watching the fabric go from dark to light, dark to light. I tapped my toe, my leg shaking automatically and without control. Had the room gotten hotter since I had sat down? She talked to me about abstinence and how she and her son's father had sought accountability from their pastor to stay abstinent. They hadn't been able to stay abstinent, and she became pregnant around 18. She encouraged me, that if I wasn't pregnant, my boyfriend and I needed to stay abstinent. Both to ensure something like this wouldn't happen again, and to please God. I nodded wholeheartedly- if I wasn't pregnant, I promised God I would never have sex before marriage again.

Her phone timer went off and I jumped up before calming myself. I could feel my heartbeat reverberating throughout my entire body- it pulsated in my ears. We somberly made our way to the bathroom and stared at the test on the counter. Two pink lines.

Two pink lines.

Two of them.

My brain was spinning as I realized everything those two lines meant for my life, for my hopes and my dreams. I would have to tell my parents I was pregnant- or *could I keep it a secret? How long could I keep it a secret? Could I finish high school? Would my parents kick me out? What would my friends think? Would I ever be able to go to college? How was I going to survive childbirth? How long did pregnancy last again? Could the test be wrong? How could this happen to someone like me?* I didn't say a word as silent tears fell from my eyes and pattered against the wood floor. His sister hugged me tightly for a long time and said over and over,

"Your life isn't over- okay? Your life isn't over, I promise." She said. That's what I would tell anyone in a similar situation now- she was right. I just couldn't see the future back then; I could only see six inches in front of me. If I could go back to scared, lonely, pregnant Kayla and show her just a glimpse of the joy and prosperity that was to come, I would. But alas, I cannot time travel.

Perhaps it is a blessing that we can't time travel, because we would spend all of our lives trying to remember every crossroad we ever approached, and going back in time to test alternate routes. Mistakes would haunt us, consume us, and maybe we would spend more time in the past than we would in the present.

It felt like my life was truly over. It felt unreal. I spent a lot of time in shock, and then in denial. It couldn't happen to me, to other people sure, but not *me*. I wasn't the type of girl who got pregnant in high school. Not me. Maybe this mentality is what got me pregnant in the first place- I never thought it could happen to me. That, and I was uneducated. I hated teen moms, they were failures, they were irresponsible. And suddenly I was one of them. I told myself that if I just didn't think about it, maybe it would un-happen. If I just pretended my life was continuing like normal, maybe it would. Maybe if I prayed hard enough and squeezed my eyes closed tight enough on my pillow at night, I would wake up and this would all go away. It would all be a bad dream, because that's what it felt like. But it wasn't that easy, and I couldn't make it go away. It was my life now.

After reality had sunken in that I was pregnant, I started feeling different. Now, with the knowledge in my head that my body was growing a baby, I could feel how hard my pelvic area was. My boobs were sore, and I was chronically fatigued and hungry. My steps felt a little heavier and my hand found its way to my belly a little more naturally. It was like an instinct. Suddenly, I felt pregnant, and I felt it throughout my whole body. *There was a baby in me.*

The day I took the first positive pregnancy test, I kept it wrapped up in the plastic Walgreens bag in my backpack. My boyfriend's sister dropped me back off at school right as the bell rang and classes were dismissed. My dad picked me up only a few minutes later to take me to my little brother's birthday party. It was at a minigolf place, and I remember secretly transferring the pregnancy test wrapped in plastic from my backpack into my jacket. I held it there while I ran to use the outhouse by the minigolf course. I dropped it in the outhouse and never looked back.

From that point I remember being unable to eat, unable to sleep, chewing on my lip incessantly, riddled with an anxiety so deep that it penetrated my soul. *My life was over. My life was over. My parents were going to kill me.* My youth pastor was at my brother's birthday party and I must have looked like I'd seen a ghost, because he later asked me if I was okay. I asked if I could talk to him alone- I *needed* to talk to somebody.

He invited me to his house the next day to talk. We made awkward small talk before going into his backyard and sitting in lawn chairs on the patio for privacy. I confessed to everything- I confessed to having sex and the details of my relationship. He listened to me and although I could see the concern in his face, he just nodded.

"I think that you need to tell your parents what you are telling me." He said.

"I don't think I have a choice." I mumbled, looking at him sadly. By now, my hand had found its way to my belly. I watched as the gears turned in his head and his face changed, as he tilted his head the slightest bit and looked at me through squinted eyes. "I'm pregnant".

After the initial shock and after praying for me, John took me inside and with my permission, told his wife Val. She was pregnant at the time and had leftover pregnancy tests. I took two in their bathroom, and to little surprise to me, they were both positive. I sat at their kitchen table, relieved that somebody knew my secret. To break the tension, I remember John awkwardly grinning and offering me a Hershey's bar that was on his counter.

"Chocolate?" I can't remember if I took it or not. John, Val, and I talked for probably an hour. I expressed my fear of telling my parents, and they agreed that they would be fearful too. They knew my parents from church and had become friends with them. We came up with a plan for them to help me break the news- they would invite my parents over the following week and be there as moral support while I told them.

"John, what do I do if her dad gets angry? What about if he gets aggressive?" Val asked. John raised an eyebrow at her.

"Then you let ME handle it, you're pregnant. You don't do anything." We chuckled nervously, but the light humor in the room only distracted me from the terror in my heart for a short while. Soon, I had to return home, to where my secret was still hidden, clandestine in my heart. The days of secrecy at home were painful and anxiety-ridden. One morning while my dad was driving me to school, I started to feel the dreaded feeling of saliva pooling in my mouth. You know the feeling I'm talking about. My stomach was starting to jump into my throat and I clenched my fists as I held back the urge to vomit. Beads of sweat formed on my forehead as I fought my body for five minutes. Somehow, miraculously, I didn't throw up. That was my only real experience of morning sickness and I remember it clearly.

When the day finally came for us to go to John and Val's house, I was the most anxious I have ever been in my entire adult life. To this day, I have never experienced such a terrorizing nervousness. Nothing has compared. They asked me on the car ride over what John could possibly want to talk to us all about- I shrugged and chewed the inside of my lip. When we arrived, my parents each sat on the couch, and I sat crisscross on the floor facing them. I let my fingers grab the thick carpet and let it go, over and over. Maybe if I grabbed it hard enough, in just the right spot, a square of the floor would rise and I could fly away on it, like Aladdin.

"Kayla has something she would like to tell you, and we are here to support her and you." John said, or something along those lines. I couldn't even speak through my tears. The air got stuck in my throat and I couldn't form words. I glanced at John and Val, hoping they would say the words for me, but they only stared at me, waiting. They weren't going to do the hard part for me. I started my sentence over and over without finishing it- instead, my eyes would get caught on the orange painting on the wall. It was monochromatic painting of a dirt path through a village. Clay buildings with clay roofs and bamboo fences lined the road. Palm trees and clouds shaped like cotton balls filled the background. I wished I could close my eyes and teleport there, just for a few moments. I imagined I would sit on the ground in the dirt and sift through the pebbles in the sand while I found the perfect words to say, words that would come out of my mouth like butter and there would be no way anyone could react negatively to what I said.

I refocused on the room I was in and choked out, "I'm pregnant". The air sat stagnant in the room for what felt like thirty minutes of silence. The only sound was my dad weeping. My parents left me there for a while so they could talk. Val exclaimed that she had expected a very different reaction, perhaps yelling or arguing. I did too, but I think the silent reaction I got was worse.

They dropped me off at home a few hours later. Before I left, Val gave me a bottle of Prenatal vitamins she bought me. When I opened the front door and entered the house, I heard a loud conversation quickly silence itself. I tried to make my way quickly to my room, but my parents intercepted me.

"Let's go for a walk." My dad said without looking at me. I pulled a jacket out of my closet and zipped it up before following them out the door. We walked down the road to the bike path. They asked me lots of questions, mostly ones like, "how did this happen?" "when did you even have sex?" "why did you do this?" "what do you think you're going to do?" and statements like "we just can't believe this." "we are so disappointed." The following few weeks at home were tense and uncomfortable. After that walk, we barely spoke. When we did speak, the words were riddled with disappointment and anger. For a long time, home felt like purgatory.

My mother littered our conversations with things like, "I thought we raised you right." And "He raped you, didn't he?" they just couldn't believe that I had disappointed them so greatly, they had to look for an outside source to blame. If it was my fault, then it reflected on their parenting, but if they could blame something or someone else, it didn't. My dad even told me, "Well, it looks like you just won't be able to come to church with us for the next nine months." That stuck with me. They took me to a Christian clinic downtown to do an ultrasound, to make sure I was truly pregnant, despite the three tests I had already taken. The ultrasound confirmed I was pregnant, and as I sat, uncomfortably exposed in a room with my Catholic mother and a vaginal probe inside my body, I saw my baby's heartbeat for the first time. For a moment I felt happy, I felt excitement. I smiled. It was a baby, a real baby. It was my baby, it was inside of me, and it was beautiful. My parents didn't think so yet. My mother did not share my happiness, and my moment of excitement was quickly diminished as the ultrasound technician printed the photos and I dressed myself silently. I argued with my parents on the drive home. I can't remember now exactly what the topics of our arguments were, but they were always conversations full of disappointment and guilt.

Once my parents knew that I was pregnant, the secret quickly spread like a wildfire through my family. One person's 'don't tell anyone' was passed on from one to another, until in a matter of days the cat was out of the bag. Pieces of conversations got passed on to me. Exclamations like,

"with whom?!", "How OLD is she? Fifteen?!" and "I had a feeling this would happen." For years I had grown up hearing whisperings of family drama- one cousin had done this to another cousin, this cousin had made this mistake, but suddenly, none of the family drama of the past even remotely compared to me getting pregnant at 15. On both sides, my mom's religious family and my dad's carefree and fun side of the family, I was the new black sheep.

Aunts and uncles would no longer trust my little cousins to spend alone time with me- though a subtle shift, I was no longer seen as a good influence. I could feel it in their eyes when they looked at me.

One day, my little brother came home from school saying his classmate had told his class that his older sister was pregnant. He was only in the fifth grade. He proudly told my parents and I that he had defended me and shut down the rumor. The clock on the wall now ticked more loudly than I had ever noticed before. The fridge whirred and began to hum as the room came alive. The colored flowers on the wallpaper above the old wooden cabinets screamed at me and the purple squares on the worn linoleum under my feet danced before my eyes. I nudged the old nick in the floor with the toe of my shoe, peeling up the corner of the flooring, and then letting it fall back into place. Finally, I looked up. My parents glared at me. My brother looked at us, confusion in his face.

"We were waiting to tell you." I whispered. He scrunched his young face in confusion, then sadness, then disgust.

"How could you do that before marriage?!" he yelled, running to his room and slamming the door, sniffling audibly. I stared at the purple squares on the floor that had stopped dancing. I went to my room and sat on my bed, staring at the wall and letting tears fall down my cheeks. It seemed like crying was now just a part of who I was- I cried so often that you'd think I would run out of tears, or the lump in my throat would hurt less, but every day it hurt the same and the tears continued to flow.

I stood up and began ripping down the notes and mall photo-strips plastered all over my old wooden door. I pulled down posters after poster and photo after photo. I turned and looked at my room, at how childish it appeared. The walls were a bright blue, my bedspread was covered in lime green circles, my bed had stuffed animals on it. A "Live Laugh Love" plaque hung on the wall. Lime green curtains fell from my window. I threw the stuffed animals under my bed and took down the curtains. I decided that I would paint, and I would paint soon. I would buy a new bedspread and new curtains, colorless ones. How could I be a mother and live in a child's bedroom?

Family wasn't the only place the news of my pregnancy quickly spread. The following few days at school felt like I was wearing a scarlet A on my shirt. Eyes that had never taken a second glance at me began to linger on me in the halls and classrooms. Perhaps part paranoia but part truth, it felt like people whispered as I passed by. I didn't have much connection to my friends anymore after isolating myself in my first relationship. It seemed like these 'friends' were the ones who whispered the most.

At first, I didn't want anyone to know that I was pregnant. I wanted to keep it a secret. I remember the first time someone mentioned it, I froze. I had just sat down in my design art class, my body tired. I leaned back against the cool metal of the seat and let my backpack sink to the floor by my feet. My body was exhausted in a way I had never felt before. A friend of my son's father was sitting nearby, and he loudly whispered,

"PSST! Kayla!" I looked over at him. "Are you really pregnant?!" he asked. The room went from quiet to silent, and everyone sitting nearby turned to stare at me. I felt the blood rush to my neck, then my face and ears.

"No, what the hell?" I scoffed, scrunching my face. I began to feel dizzy as the temperature in the room seemingly raised by 10 degrees. Luckily, the teacher called everyone's attention, and the moment passed as quickly as it had begun. My face stayed red and my heart continued to pound in my chest for another few minutes after everyone else had forgotten what had happened. I wondered if the teacher had heard- I hoped not. I really liked her.

More days than not, I texted my parents and begged them to pick me up early from school. Drama followed me throughout my day, partially because of old friends, partially because my secret was spreading like wildfire, partially because people kept coming right up and asking me about it, and partially because I was amidst my first breakup with my unborn baby's father, who also attended the same school as me. Life got messy.

My dad often came to my rescue, pulling up to the front of the school in the grey minivan like the Batmobile had just arrived to save me. Most days I had to decide which situation was more uncomfortable- being at school or being with my parents, who were still barely speaking to me. It really depended on the day.

As I remember, I was the first (at least in a while) pregnant teenager at my traditional high school. Because of this, my counselor told me that I needed to transfer schools to the alternative high school with a program for teen moms- so I did. Both because I was under the impression that I had to, and to escape inevitable breakup drama. I quickly discovered that this alternative school didn't offer any math past Algebra 2, any Spanish past Spanish 1, had teachers teaching 2-3 subjects each, and absolutely no incentive or preparation for its students to pursue secondary education. However, the school reminded me that I would not be allowed to use the district's free childcare for teen parents unless I attended *their* school and *their* pregnancy class. As a solution, I spent several months of my pregnancy between two schools- neither of which were my original high school. Instead, I spent the mornings at the nearby traditional high school taking the advanced classes not offered by the alternative school, caught a bus during lunch hour to the alternative school, and took the pregnancy class and P.E. there in the afternoons. This was, in the eyes of myself and my parents, a way to still get the childcare once my baby was born, and still get a good education.

Before I had gotten pregnant, I was an honor student with dreams of college. One thing I am eternally grateful to my parents for, is that they decided that my getting pregnant was NOT going to ruin my dreams for my life. After months of this daily transfer between two schools (neither of which I had any friends at, other than the few pregnant girls that were kind to me), I was depressed and exhausted. I missed my best friend at my original high school. I spent my lunch hours eating a sack lunch on the curb behind the school, waiting for the bus to pick me up. I would walk the halls during breaks and pretend like I had somewhere to go- always walking quickly, trying to act busy, just to kill time and not look alone. People stared, people pointed, and the larger my belly got, the more I stood out. If you've ever experienced being the new girl at a new school, imagine being the new pregnant girl. I'm sure everybody had their own fantasies they made up in their heads about where I came from and what happened to me.

One of my old friends from middle school went to this new high school, and she noticed me when I transferred. Sometimes she invited me to eat lunch with her friend group in the cafeteria or hang out in the library. In the beginning, I don't think she realized I was pregnant. I never told her, I just assumed she realized.

One of my old youth group leaders from church worked as the campus hall monitor, so occasionally he would pull me out of class and just let me sit in his office and talk. If I was having a hard day, I could text him and ask him to pull me out of class, and magically, someone from the office would deliver the little yellow paper to my teacher.

I was sitting in history class at this school when I very first felt the baby kick. At first, when a pregnant mother feels movement from her child, it feels like gas bubbles or like nervous butterflies. When I finally felt an undeniable flutter in my abdomen in class, I held my stomach tightly under my jacket with my hand, and I held back tears of joy. I don't think I took in any of the material that we learned in class that day, because I spent the rest of the class clutching my stomach and hoping to feel the flutters again. I wished I was somewhere where I could proclaim my excitement or let someone feel the kicks with me, but I was sitting in class and the moment couldn't be very romanticized. This was the first of many important milestones that I cherished alone.

When I had transferred between my original high school and the two new schools, I had missed a week or two of school during the process. Because of this, I fell behind in math and science. I had always been a year advanced and school had always come easily to me, but once I fell behind in Chemistry and Trigonometry, I was completely lost. I spent many days after school making up Chemistry labs. Once my dad picked me up from the alternative school, I would have him drive me back to the other school. I spent hours trying to catch up, but for some reason, it never clicked. Maybe it was a result of my mind being constantly scattered and the amount of stress I was dealing with, but I remember being completely devastated to find out that the teacher only gave me a D+. It was my first non-passing grade I had ever received, and it felt unfair because of how hard I was trying. My math grade was similar, and for the first time in my life, I no longer felt smart. I felt stupid. So, for the remainder of the semester, I minded my own business, did my schoolwork, and went home. Each day when my dad would pick me up, it was a relief.

After discussing how it didn't make sense that the school district would seemingly inhibit my academic potential in order to provide me with childcare, my parents and I advocated for my right to a traditional education at the Superintendent's office. To my joy, I was granted permission to return full time to my original high school, and still access the district's childcare. Although ecstatic for myself, I couldn't help but feel a little uneasy about the other teen moms I had met and befriended at the alternative school. The district and the alternative school pressured us to be very quiet about our agreement- they didn't want the other teen moms having the same idea.

Although there is sense in requiring teen moms to attend a parenting program to access free childcare, I found it degrading that the only option they had was to attend this program at an alternative school that offered no college preparatory courses, had only a handful of teachers, and was mostly full of the students who had been expelled from the traditional schools. My experiences in those classrooms were ones of shock at the way that students disrespected the teachers- daily cursing out of instructors, kids being sent out of class, hallway fights, principal entrances into classrooms to pull out students, campus arrests, and students smoking outside between every class. I had grown up (surprisingly, I know) in a strict, religious household. I was completely sheltered. I had never felt so out of place as I did at that school.

So, with an aching heart for the teen moms I left behind who didn't have the same opportunity as me, I returned to my school. My return was not triumphant- most of my long-time friends that I had since elementary school stopped talking to me. I (and my relationship with my son's father) had become somewhat of a joke between the people I had once thought were my best friends. My old cheer coaches wouldn't make eye contact with me in the hallways anymore.

Of course, I had one best friend who stuck by my side through it all, and for whom I am eternally grateful. Despite feeling like an outcast, at least I had her. She was still a cheerleader, she was still a normal teenager, but she never made me feel like a misfit. She balanced both sides of her life- her normal teenage girl side, and the side of her that helped me look at cribs, change

47

diapers, go on walks with the stroller, and sit at home with a baby all day.

When I got pregnant, not only did I lose friends, but my friends' parents disapproved of me as well. They didn't want their kids to hang out with me because I was now seen as a bad influence, as a troublemaker, a delinquent. Parents told their daughters not to be like me and told their sons not to date girls like me. Adults who had known my parents since we had all gone to elementary school together suddenly avoided eye contact with me and my parents at school events. I even got inducted into the National Honor Society while I was pregnant, along with many of my old friends and classmates for 9+ years. All the parents were there, watching our names get called as we walked across the stage. Hearing my name called and waddling my pregnant self across that stage to get my certificate was both embarrassing and liberating. It felt good knowing I was proving all those parents wrong, that I was sitting in the *same place* as their kids, despite my circumstances.

My most vivid memories of being pregnant in high school came from being back at the school where I had started. I knew everybody and soon everybody knew me. As my belly grew, so did the rest of my body. Towards the end of my last trimester, my feet and ankles were so swollen that the only shoes I could wear to school were flip flops. By the end of the day, my flip flops left lines indented in my swollen feet. I remember being self-conscious that people were looking at my swollen feet in class, and I don't doubt they were. When I say that my swelling was bad, I mean it was *bad.* I've always been curious to research how pregnancy affects the body of a teenager differently than the body of a grown woman. Maybe if I get pregnant again someday, I can compare the pregnancies.

My backpack felt like it was close to thirty pounds, but I had no choice but to carry all my textbooks around in it all day. I had transferred back too late in the school year to get a locker, and I didn't drive myself to school to have a car to leave them in. I'm sure that my body was three feet in length from the tip of my stomach to the end of my backpack, but people always seemed to give me enough space in the hallways to walk. Maybe they thought pregnancy was contagious, or they thought I would run them over. Regardless, nobody seemed to get in my way.

My favorite class I took while pregnant was my drawing class. The teacher was a laid-back hippie who played his guitar during class and let students work ultimately at their own pace. His classroom was on the farthest end of the campus in the detached art/mechanics building. The room was full of large tables and eight students could sit at each table. The walls were plastered with artwork from past students and posters from the 60s. In the back of the room was an old record player, which the teacher would use to play records during class when he wasn't playing his guitar. Next to the record player was an old boxy computer, an Apple from before I was born. He offered to teach students digital art if they were interested, but I was always skeptical what kind of art software that machine could handle. The art room was attached by a door to the shop where the mechanics classes were taught. When that room was empty, he would let me work alone out there at a singular table.

Students often took his art classes because they thought it was an easy A. I took his art classes because I loved art. Ever since I was a little girl, I had always spent all of my free time drawing. Every birthday and every Christmas resulted in a new sketchbook and pencils, most of which were never filled in completely by the time I moved on to the next.

When I was young, my parents somehow became the owners of an old typewriter. I don't remember where they got it, but it became my favorite possession. I spent hours upon hours typing my own stories, stapling the papers together, and then illustrating the stories I had written. Before long I had my own little library of my own novels, a bookshelf full of hand-typed and hand-illustrated stories on stapled together pieces of printer paper. When I wasn't writing or drawing, I was reading. I spent a lot of time alone in my bedroom growing up, and maybe that has some impact on my level of introversion as an adult. Growing up with only my brother, who spent all his time in solidarity, made me feel like an only child.

In high school art, the teacher noticed my passion for art and my ability to quickly complete his simple drawing assignments. Soon, I had my own raised table and a set of pastel chalks in front of me. He always pushed me. I always had my own assignments and I got to use his personal sets of art supplies from his office, and he even let me work in the empty side room if I wanted to escape the noisy classroom. Sometimes it felt like he was only taking pity on me because I was pregnant, but I honestly didn't mind it. If I told him I was hungry, he let me leave class to go buy food. If I told him I needed the bathroom pass three times in one hour, he didn't question me.

I in fact became quite close with this teacher even after my son was born. I repeated his intro to drawing class every single semester until I graduated and worked independently on my own art projects. After graduation, he gave me his contact information and visited my art booth at the local Saturday Market. In some ways, he was my art mentor when I needed someone most. At a time when most of the adults in my life were angry and disappointed in me, he was there for me. He didn't see me as a pregnant girl, he saw me as a student with potential. During this time, I decided I wanted to be an art teacher, so that I could help students escape through art. Escape bad home lives, escape stress, escape reality, even if just for one class period. I wanted to help other kids channel their emotions through art, like he helped me do. Art class was my escape.

For the most part, my teachers were kind and understanding. One day I even walked into class a little early to witness my writing teacher swapping my assigned desk for a larger one- I'm sure he had seen me struggling to fit in my seat the day before. My math teacher let me leave class to get snacks and coffee, although I'm sure he would deny it now if his job depended on it. There was an unwritten agreement with most of my teachers, that they just understood. They understood that school was harder for me, that my body was exhausted, and that I was humiliated by it all. They never called on me unprovoked, they let me sit in the back, and they were understanding if I had to miss class for appointments.

Now, notice I said *most*. There was one teacher who was an exception. I couldn't figure out if he didn't realize he was embarrassing me or if he liked doing so. He sat me right up front in the center of the classroom. He questioned everything I turned in, every appointment I had to miss class for, and wouldn't let me make up any work I had to miss. The bathroom was the worst part. His class was in the afternoon, right after lunch. As my pregnancy progressed, my need to use the restroom rapidly increased. I was going pee every hour, if not more. His class was an hour and a half, and there was no way I could make it through the entire period without using the bathroom. I tried, many times, until I was in physical pain.

Many of his classes were just us watching films of conspiracy theories he believed in. He had a rule-nobody left class during the film. At one point, I could no longer hold my bladder as the baby bounced on it, and I quickly stood and walked to his desk, ducking in front of the TV. I hated being in front of people, so I wouldn't have done that if I didn't absolutely have to.

"May I please go to the restroom?" I whispered. He looked up at me, his face emotionless.

"Can't you wait until the end of the video like everyone else?" He did *not* whisper. Now, it felt like every eye was on me. Maybe I remember it being more traumatizing than it was, but I remember shamefully shaking my head no. I could not, I literally could not wait. I was seconds away from peeing my pants in front of the class. He let out a loud exhale and handed me the hall pass. "Be fast." I left that classroom as quickly as I could.

In addition to always needing to use the restroom, I found myself always hungry. I would eat a big breakfast in the morning, pack a lunch, and by 9:30 am I had already nibbled away all my sandwich and eaten everything from my lunch that wouldn't make noise in class. During the break between classes, I always went to the coffee cart on campus. The only food I could buy there were warm, freshly baked chocolate chip cookies, and they were amazing. However, eating a 3 pack of homemade chocolate cookies every day likely contributed to my excessive weight gain. But I was starving, what else could I do?

Usually when the baby kicked in class, everyone was facing forward so nobody noticed. I loved when he did that- it was like a little mental escape from learning to place my hand on my belly and remember the reason I was there. One of the classes I took during my pregnancy was theatre. It was just an introductory theatre class, so most of my old friends weren't in it. But my best friend took it with me, and we loved our theatre teacher. In this class, we often sat in chairs in a big circle on stage for activities or reading of scripts out loud. One day, the baby went crazy in my stomach. Flipping, kicking, turning, so quickly and drastically that my stomach looked inhuman.

"Whoa!" someone said, pointing. Now, everyone in the circle was staring at my stomach as it contorted itself in different shapes. My teacher even laughed and gave us all permission to focus on my belly for a few minutes. A few students asked if they could touch it, and I said yes. Peers I barely knew placed their hands on my stomach and 'ooh'ed and 'aww'ed at the amazing phenomena of a human moving inside of me. That was one of the only times I wasn't embarrassed to be the center of attention.

One day as my best friend and I walked into the cafeteria, three of the most popular girls in my grade walked up to us. They asked if they could touch my belly, and I said sure, because how could I say no to them? These girls had never said a word to me in my life, and I was shocked that they even knew my name. When they walked away, my best friend and I looked at each other and laughed together about how weird that was.

I rode the school bus home most days with my best friend- we lived a few blocks away and were only one bus stop apart. Our stops were the last two stops, so the bus ride was nearly an hour, but I didn't mind.

Anything to avoid the tension of being at home with my parents. For this reason, also, I spent a lot of time at my youth pastor's house. Once his wife had their baby, I came over often to get 'baby experience'. They even paid me to babysit every Thursday night while they hosted a bible study at their house. This was truly the first experience I really had with a baby. I had never babysat young kids before and now I was expecting my own.

I spent my evenings setting up my son's nursery, which was basically just a corner of my bedroom. I re-painted our room twice, with the help of my best friend. My sixteenth birthday was in fact spent painting the room with her and then eating cake with my family. There's no Sweet Sixteen birthday party when you're a pregnant teenager.

Being that I was only fifteen, I couldn't drive myself to any of my doctor appointments. So, my mom took me to most of them. This only added to how uncomfortable I was as a fifteen-year-old at her first OBGYN office. Most appointments we sat in silence until the doctor arrived. I remember my first time meeting my Obstetrician, she asked me if I had been using any method of birth control when I got pregnant. Before I could answer, my mom responded for me, "No, we thought we had raised her right and she wouldn't have sex before marriage, but apparently not." I think this surprised the doctor as much as me, because I shrunk in my chair and the doctor quickly changed the subject.

My parents forced me to take a birthing class at the local hospital, of course, with good intentions. I insisted that my pregnancy class at the alternative school had already prepared me for childbirth (and it really had), but they insisted. As my mom and I entered the room, it didn't take long for me to notice that I was different from everyone else in two major ways: First, I was younger than everyone by at least ten years, and second, I was the ONLY one there with their mother. Every other expectant mother there was with her partner, and I was there with my mom. I was humiliated. We did simulation breathing and labor exercises, and every time she had to hold me or touch me, I held my breath. I was so angry and embarrassed. I wanted nothing more than to run out of the room and run home. My face hot, I held back tears until the 6-hour class ended, we got home, and I could lock myself in my bedroom.

After finding out I was pregnant, my parents privately talked to the head pastor. He reassured them that the church would continue to love and support me, so I kept going. Although I received mixed reactions from different people, I was shocked by the amount of support and love I received. Not everyone was kind- my dad's friend asked him, "What is she going to do? What does she think it is, a DOLL?" My middle school youth leader, whom I had spent much of my summers at her house with her family and looked up to, unfriended me on Facebook. Interactions like those made me ashamed, but they didn't compare to the love and support I received. To my surprise, my youth pastor's wife and some women from the church threw me a baby shower. Anticipating a low turnout, I was nervous and embarrassed to show up. I was wrong- the room was absolutely packed. I received more gifts than I could have imagined, and I had never been more grateful. People anonymously gifted me large items like stroller/car seat sets and generous gift cards. By the time I was 40 weeks pregnant, I had everything I needed for my baby's arrival, and it had all been given to me.

During my pregnancy, one of the elders at my church offered for me to attend his Financial Peace University class he was leading- it was a Dave Ramsey class about handling your finances and building wealth. He paid for my class, workbook and materials. After a few weeks of the class, I was feeling motivated to set myself up for financial success. Being only 15, I didn't have a job yet, so I didn't really have a way to make money, but I wanted to start saving. Most employers in Oregon required that employees be 16 years of age, so I would keep my eye out on Craigslist and occasionally the newspaper classified ads for babysitting jobs or odd work.

One day, I saw an ad in the newspaper (ironically) for a part-time job for youth selling newspaper subscriptions through an Oregon newspaper group. The ad said something like *'Earn $100-400 per week!'* I signed up immediately. The first evening, a big white van pulled up to my house to pick me up. My parents were extremely skeptical- they went out and introduced themselves to the man in charge, who must have identified himself as someone important and trustworthy. They let me go. The van was full of random kids- some around 13, some my age, some looking closer to 18. The van went around picking everyone up as the driver gave us his sales pitch- we would get paid a dollar amount for every newspaper subscription we sold. If we hit the goal number of subscriptions for the night, we would get a $100 bonus. He paid us in cash at the end of every night. It seemed like an easy way to make money, although in retrospect it was super sketchy. I'd never let my son get in a random white van that pulled up to the house at 6 pm.

Luckily, the whole operation was legitimate and I didn't end up kidnapped or murdered. Each evening (I believe we went twice a week) the van would pick all of us up and drop us off in a neighborhood. We would each take a side of a street, divvying up the area between us. We walked and knocked on doors, pitching to people why they should want the Register Guard Newspaper delivered to their house each week. Fall was just transitioning to Winter when I began, and I remember the nights quickly became rigidly cold. I started to notice that people's eyes were drawn to my belly when I spoke to them- and I totally milked it. The man in charge even told us to tell people we were working towards earning college scholarships. I never saw anything about a scholarship, but I sure told people I was earning one. Maybe I should have pursued a career as a professional scammer. (Joke).

For some reason, maybe because I was a little pregnant girl knocking on doors in the dark on frozen nights, I had the highest number of sales almost every night. I signed up person after person, often earning the bonus of the day and stuffing it in my savings jar when I got home. I remember evenings where my toes were painfully frozen in my shoes as I trudged along the icy road, from door to door to door, selling newspaper subscriptions in the dark.

Eventually, because I had such good sales, they asked me if I would want to sit at a table in the entryway of the local Fred Meyer. I said yes because I wanted the money. I had a baby on the way and was too young to get a real job. I set up every week at that table in between the sliding glass doors at the Springfield Fred Meyer, saying "Newspaper Subscriptions!" as people walked in and out. I was often embarrassed by seeing people I knew- how much more could I stand out like a sore thumb than being fifteen, pregnant, *and* trying to sell newspapers to people as they went to buy groceries? Eventually, I got too pregnant to manage sitting there for the 8 hours/day that this newspaper sales group wanted me to. The days were long and I wasn't selling as many subscriptions. I eventually quit, and kept my little nest egg mason jar of cash to buy things for my coming baby.

I had my son in May of my sophomore year. I named him Landon and he immediately became the brightest light of my life. I was four days past due when I was finally induced, on prom night. I remember this detail because I cut out a little paper necktie and taped it to my belly for a photo before we left for the hospital. I posted it on my Instagram with some caption about the baby being my prom date. I scrolled through my newsfeed to pass the time before leaving for the hospital, looking at all of my friends in their beautiful dresses and their normal bodies. They had dates, they went to fancy dinners, and some rented limos to take them from dinner to the dance. I wasn't an upperclassman yet, so only my friends who had been asked to the dance by older dates went- but it seemed like that was a lot of them. I tried to imagine what I'd look like in a prom dress with my huge protruding belly- I probably wouldn't fit in any prom dresses at all.

Besides, who would have asked the pregnant sophomore to prom?

I was induced at 11 pm that night and had an emergency C-section the next day after mine and Landon's heart rates had dropped from pushing. My parents had left to go get food in the cafeteria, since I wasn't even 7 centimeters dilated yet. While they were gone, our heart rates dropped, and the doctor told me to start pushing. I tried to push, but I wasn't dilated enough, so they began to hurriedly prepare me for a C-section. My parents told me that there was a red light flashing outside my room and nurses wouldn't let them in- they were terrified. From the inside, I didn't realize the urgency of the situation because of how calm everyone was. By the time they wheeled me to the room where the procedure would happen, my mom was allowed to get dressed in scrubs and a mask to join me. I had already had an epidural line in my spine, so luckily I was able to be conscious when my son was born. They simply put the anesthetics in the already administered line. Nurses later told my parents that, without modern technology, neither my son or I would have survived childbirth with the circumstances. I wondered if my age had anything to do with it. The anesthesiologist asked me if I wanted him to take photos over the curtain with my iPhone and I said yes. I still have those iPhone photos of Landon being pulled out of my giant stomach-hole. Landon thinks they're awesome and says he kind of looked like an alien. He's not wrong.

When babies are born, they are given an APGAR score. Apgar stands for "Appearance, Pulse, Grimace, Activity, and Respiration." Each is scored on a scale of 0 to 2, with 2 being the best score. So, a perfect APGAR score is 10, and you can figure out what a 0 means. When Landon was born, his APGAR score was 1 out of 10. As soon as they pulled him out, they whisked him away to pump his lungs. I laid there, frozen in fear, praying as hard as I could that I would hear a cry. I clenched my interlocked fingers together until my knuckles were white and I pleaded with God in my head. Tears fell from my tightly closed eyes as I tuned out the hum of organized chaos in the room- *please, God, please, please, I will do anything, please let my son be alive. Please. Please, please, I have never asked for anything so deeply and I will never ask another favor again, please. Please. Please. Please save my baby. Please God please.* My body trembled as I listened for a sound other than the whirring of machines and doctors and nurses working on stitching me back up.

Finally, I heard a wailing cry. He was 8 pounds, 1 ounce and had the finest blonde hair on his head. At first, because it was wet, I thought it was curly. I loved it. Then it dried and it was straight- and I still loved it. It wouldn't have mattered what he looked like; I would have loved him unconditionally with my whole heart no matter what. Meeting the mysterious baby that I had felt growing and living inside of my body for months was the most surreal and joyful experience of my life. It instantly washed over every tear I had shed, every stressful moment, every negative comment from my peers, and every fear. It triumphed over every single bad day I had ever experienced- I would do it all over again, tenfold, in a heartbeat, for him. I wish I could relive that day over again a thousand times. I can't wait to have more babies.

I finished the remainder of the school year by coming to class once a week and taking home my schoolwork. My teachers were more than gracious and always understanding. I remember the last month of the school year being a strange experience, as I transitioned from being the pregnant girl to just being another girl in the crowded hallways. I didn't have to waddle, my stomach didn't lead me by a foot's distance, and I fit in my desks again. I was breastfeeding and by the time my 1.5-hour classes were done, I was engorged and in pain. There was nowhere for me to plug in an electric breast pump at school unless I wanted to pump in the health room, which was openly exposed to the back part of the school office where student aids and administration were constantly walking through. So, I brought a small hand pump in my backpack, and when the pain got bad enough, I would sit in a bathroom stall, handpump enough milk to relieve the pain, and dump it in the toilet. This was frustrating to do, as any breastfeeding mom can understand, because that stuff is liquid gold. However, I didn't have anywhere to store the milk or keep it cold, and I always feared having some freak accident where breastmilk would leak from my backpack in class and everyone would point and scream. So, at school I pumped and dumped.

One day in particular, I was sitting on the edge of the toilet seat, hand cramping from pumping breast milk, as I listened to other girls in the bathroom discuss what their homecoming dresses looked like. They talked about their dinner plans before homecoming, whose house they would get ready at, and their dates. Suddenly it hit me, that I was pumping breastmilk on a toilet while my peers planned their exciting homecoming night. Their bodies weren't too big to fit in the dress they wanted to wear, they had dates because boys still liked them, they wouldn't have to leave the dance halfway through to pump breastmilk, and they had no idea I was even in the bathroom. I felt invisible. Or, more so I felt like an outsider, like an alien. *I didn't know what it was like to be a high school girl anymore.*

After summer break, I decided to try doing online school so I could stay home with Landon and continue to breastfeed. I did this for the first half of my junior year, until I became sick of it. I missed school, I missed seeing my best friend every day, and I was lonely from being home alone all day while my parents and my brother were gone. I returned to my high school for the second half of my junior year and Landon went to the district childcare while I had class (per my secret arrangement with the school district). I continued to pump and provide breastmilk to the daycare until my supply ran low and I realized I was exhausting myself. Ashamedly, I switched to giving Landon formula when he was about 8 months old.

The rest of my high school experience was standard- or at least standard for MY reality. As my body returned to my pre-baby weight (I had gained fifty pounds during my pregnancy, all of which was NOT the baby, or else I would have capitalized off of Ripley's Believe it or Not or something for a fifty-pound newborn). I began to feel a little more normal. I joked about myself being a teen mom before my peers could, and people laughed. On the first day of class my senior year, my teacher had every student say something they were good at. For whatever reason, I said,

"My name is Kayla and I'm really good at changing diapers." my classmates laughed with me, and the teacher was confused. People were nice to me, or at least to my face. There were always whisperings that would get back to me through the grapevine, calling me the "Baby Mama of Thurston High" or saying that I used my son to get attention online. For the most part I brushed it off. I even started dating again.

My senior year, I got asked to prom by my new boyfriend. He took Landon and I out to ice cream and snuck a handwritten note in Landon's shirt pocket, with some backwards and crooked letters, saying 'Will you go to prom with mommy?' I said yes and I posted a photo on Facebook of my son holding the note, since I thought it was sweet. The high school somehow saw my post and it was selected for the "Cutest Prom-Posal" contest winner. I was shocked and happy, until the backlash from parents began to reach the school administration. Parents complained that the school was endorsing teen pregnancy and that I was undeserving of winning the contest. One parent was extremely upset that her own daughter hadn't won. A few weeks later I saw this mother volunteering in the College & Career Center, and I confronted her. I apologized for any misunderstanding and clarified that I was in no way trying to promote teen pregnancy. I told her I recognized her from going to church with my parents, and she was shocked. She stuttered and denied ever complaining- and said she hadn't realized I was my parents' daughter. It was obvious that she never expected to meet me or have a conversation with me in person. Although I am hardly ever confrontational, that conversation left me with a racing heart and an empowered soul.

I finished my sophomore, junior, and senior years as a mom. My senior year, I spent my free period in the library every day applying for every scholarship I could. The College & Career Advisor in the library and I became close as she helped me apply for colleges, scholarships, and prepare for interviews. I worked the closing shift 3-4 nights per week at Five Guys, graduated with honors, and to my incredible disbelief, I was selected as a Ford Scholar by the Ford Family Foundation to receive a scholarship to any university in Oregon.

My joy was quickly interrupted as my peers began to complain about my selection for the scholarship. They said things like "she doesn't deserve it," "she's not even in AP classes", and the one that stuck with me most, "She only got that scholarship because she got knocked up." In fact, I believed those things. I began to believe that without my story of being a teen parent, I likely wouldn't have been selected as one of 100 scholars from 5,000 applicants. Out of all the scholars selected, I was the *only* one that was a parent. Regardless, the idea that I was undeserving of such an award stuck with me through college, and still does to this day. I will always wonder if I would have been selected for the scholarship if I was just a normal teenager, but it's no use to focus on what-ifs. Hell, the other scholar selected from my high school was our Valedictorian, and he sure didn't have a kid.

My freshman year of college, I went to classes during the day and worked most evenings at Dutch Bros Coffee. I made the mistake of taking an 8 am cycling class, so I would get my son ready for daycare at 6:30 am, drop him off at 7:00, drive 15 minutes to campus, spend 20 minutes trying to find parking, and then walk to class. I had a few big gaps between my classes and usually got done around 3:00 pm, when I would pick my son up from daycare and take him home. I would spend an hour or so playing with him, before leaving for my 4:45 shift at the coffee shop. My boyfriend (the same promposal boyfriend), who we lived with at the time, was incredible at helping me. The evenings I worked, he would happily send me off, make my son dinner, watch him, get him ready for bed, and put him to sleep. I'd get home around 11:30 pm, go to bed, and wake up at 6:00 to do it all again the next day. I hated this routine. I felt like I never got to see my son, like I was missing out on his life. But society said going to college was the right thing to do, so I did it.

My sophomore year of college I transitioned from working at the coffee shop to working as an office assistant at the Ford Scholarship Office. They worked around my school schedule and I quickly became close with the staff. I loved being a part of the selection process for future scholars and being able to feel like I was a part of changing lives.

College was hard. I was constantly juggling my effort between my parenting, my full-time school schedule, work, homework, being a youth leader at my church, and having a social life. I stayed up late almost every night when my son went to bed, always finishing my homework right before the deadline. I hardly slept and I was terrible at time management. My classmates always seemed so carefree, always talking about Sorority events, their dorm mates, and parties. Oh, what different lives we lived. Not to say that I did not have freedom on the days my son was with his dad- and I did go through a phase of drinking and going to parties with my friends. But each late night left me riddled with guilt, wondering what my son was doing at that moment and feeling disgustingly irresponsible. Yet, every time I promised myself I would never drink again, I always found myself with my roommates on Friday nights making plans to go out. I was still a young person- I still wanted to have fun. Being a mom didn't make that part of me go away, it just made me feel guilty for it.

In 2019 I graduated from the University of Oregon with my Bachelor of Art in Spanish, not exactly sure what I was going to do with it but content that I got a degree. According to the CDC, less than 2% of teen parents earn a college degree by the age of 30 and 90% of teen moms never graduate high school, so I was thrilled to have beat that statistic. In fact, my entire goal for the prior seven years had simply been to beat that statistic and get a degree- I hadn't really planned what would happen afterwards.

I have wanted to write a book for years, but I always procrastinated starting because I felt like I hadn't reached "the end" yet. However, I have come to realize that there is no "end". Life will always continue to flow and every ending is also a new beginning. After I publish this book, I will probably start a new beginning, and again five years after that. There will never be a time when I can look back and say that my story as a teen mom has ended, so why wait to write my story?

So, now that you know the basics of my personal story up until this point, I am going to transition to discussing specific aspects of my adult life that will be forever impacted by me being a teen mom. My suspicion is that some might be true for other teen moms as well.

## FAMILY RELATIONSHIPS

For teen moms who came from a family like mine, I would assume that their pregnancy had a huge impact on their relationships with their parents. Like I mentioned previously, I was raised in a strict Christian household. My mom was raised Catholic and I grew up in church. Although my parents were my main source of support towards the end of my pregnancy and after Landon's birth, our relationship was very strained in the beginning and is still affected by that.

My relationship with my dad wasn't as harmed by my pregnancy as my relationship with my mom- it was no secret that my dad wasn't religious when he met my mom, and he had sex before marriage. He was more understanding once the initial shock wore off. He talked to me about relationships from his past, he related his teenage years to mine and he forgave me. That was the most significant part- he forgave me much sooner than my mom did.

Now, by the time Landon was born, my parents and I acted as a more cohesive unit. My mom helped me endlessly, stayed up through the nights, helped me breastfeed, gave me breaks to rest while I did homework, and watched Landon so I could go do things. To this day, she is a tremendous help and a wonderful grandmother. Time healed many wounds, and I'm sure that more time will heal more.

After I had my son, there was a strange and subtle shift in the dynamic between my parents and I. Suddenly I was a parent too. How could they tell me where I could and couldn't go, when I was raising a young child and had to grow up immediately? It was like an unspoken emancipation; the strict rules slowly dissipated as I was, by an unspoken agreement, now an adult. I just told them where I was going and when they could expect me home. It was a strange combination of being both child and parent. Major decisions needed their permission while I had pretty much complete freedom in my day-to-day life. I could schedule and take my son to his doctor's appointments alone, but I wasn't allowed to drive myself to the coast an hour away. Sometimes this frustrated me.

My parents in fact helped me raise my son for the first three years of his life- partially because I lived in their house and it was inevitable for them to play some sort of parental role, and partially because they are truly great parents. They helped in every way they could, and this was something I felt guilty of for years. Although I couldn't move out when Landon was born because I was a minor and in high school, I hated the idea of being a stereotypical teen mom whose parents did the parenting for her. When Landon began speaking his first words, he called both my mother and I "mama". I absolutely hated it. It embarrassed me in public. Although there was a slight difference in the pronunciation and my family could tell which "mama" he was asking for, strangers did not, and I'm sure many strangers thought that Landon's grandmother was his mother.

Now, as I navigate life as a twenty-three-year-old, I am finding myself struggling with many basic aspects of life and realizing that many of them may be direct results of the way I was raised- that seems obvious, right? I never studied Psychology, but it seems like common knowledge that one's upbringing impacts the deepest fibers of their being, shaping exactly what kind of adult they become. This concept scares me as a parent, because I am already constantly pondering how I am affecting my son's identity. I wonder what baggage he will carry because of me- I wonder what book he could write about his childhood someday.

One realization I have recently come to is that I struggle to interact with adults who do not fit the mold of my parents. I grew up around strict adults who, for the most part (during my childhood), did not drink, did not curse, did not smoke, did not make inappropriate jokes, and did not discuss sex or drugs. We went to church twice per week: Once on Sunday morning and once on Wednesday evening. I grew up on Veggie Tales and Sunday School songs. When I went to extended family events, the same applied. My cousins (on my mom's side of the family at least; I rarely saw my dad's extended family) were also raised religiously. Until I began making friends who had very different home lives than me in middle school, I was relatively unexposed to much of the real world. I think my parents would even agree now that my brother and I lived a very sheltered childhood.

Now, as I make my way through life as an adult, I am often introduced to adults who are nothing like the adults I knew growing up. I've always filtered myself between the Kayla I am around my friends and the Kayla I am around adults- didn't we all? Now I'm realizing we didn't. Some people grew up without needing to have two versions of themselves- they were the same person around their friends as they were around their parents, and I have struggled to comprehend that concept. I'm sure as a teenager I would have loved to have parents I could curse, drink, and smoke with- but I didn't, so that concept is foreign to me. It's taken some adjusting to the real world to realize how different my childhood was from many of the people closest to me.

I also strive to earn approval from adults around me. Trying to overcome feeling like a disappointment turned me into a perfectionist with a deep desire for people to be proud of me. I try to earn people's approval and love, with friends, at work, in relationships, everywhere. I'm always worried about disappointing people. This is part of the reason that, after disappointing my family by getting pregnant, I was so determined to make them proud by being successful. I am always worried about people being mad at me, and I'm always asking them if they are upset. Most of the time, they aren't, until I ask them ten times, and then they *are* annoyed from my asking.

Many of the teen moms I have met struggled with their family relationships after breaking the news of their pregnancy. Quite a few of the girls I met at the alternative school had been kicked out because of it. Although my relationship with my parents was rocky, I can't imagine how much more difficult it must be to be a new mother and no longer have any contact with your family at all. Not only does this cause a wound for the young mom, but it inhibits a relationship between their child and their grandparents.

## ME VS. THEM

As a young mom I became absolutely fixated on the notion that I would be the opposite of every other teen mom. Meeting teen moms at the alternative high school who had dropped out, turned to drugs, and spent their weekends partying instead of watching their kids made me form an obsession with NOT being a teen mom. For a while, I refused to call myself one because I told myself I was simply a young parent. Before my son was even born, I had planned what I would post on Facebook when I beat the statistic and graduated high school- I planned what I would say if I was ever asked to give a speech to teen moms, I viewed myself as superior. I attributed it to my own work ethic, my morals, and my intelligence. In hindsight, I could not be more embarrassed to have felt these things.

After years of being a teen mother and reflecting upon my experience and that of others, I have come to realize that my relative 'success' is only to be attributed to one thing; I was *privileged*. I began to hear stories

86

from the other teen moms, to read Facebook posts, to run into them in public, and to see that their lives looked very different from mine, even far before they ever became pregnant teenagers. Here are some of the reasons I was able to graduate college four years after high school, despite being a teen parent:

**1.    My parents didn't kick me out when I got pregnant.**

Many of the young moms I came to know were kicked out of their parent's homes when they revealed that they were pregnant. If you think it's hard being a pregnant sixteen-year-old, imagine being a homeless pregnant sixteen-year-old. Imagine stressing about a place to live and a place to raise your child. Imagine posting on Facebook about needing a place to live- and yes, I witnessed these posts many times. Also, imagine needing to pay rent as a single parent still in high school. I knew mothers who were attending high school full-time, working 30+ hours per week at Carl's Jr., doing homework in the evenings, paying rent, and somehow finding time to be a single mom. I never asked the details about their childcare source or how they managed to do it- but as I saw from the rate of teen moms who didn't finish school, it was apparent that they became exhausted very quickly. It just didn't make sense for them to continue school, and if I were in their situation, I likely wouldn't have either.

## 2.      I had my own transportation.

Until I got my driver's license, my parents drove me to and from school every single day. Once I got my license, my parents bought me a 1999 VW Jetta. It wasn't anything luxurious, but it was a car, and that was more than many of my peers had. All I had to do in the mornings was pack my backpack, my son's diaper bag, load him in the car, and head to school. If I had to add another hour before and after school to walk to a bus stop, wait for a bus, collapse my stroller and hold my son through dozens of bus stops before I could get to his daycare, and then catch another bus to school, I would have been much less eager to go. Most of the teen parents I knew did this, every day, before and after school.

**3.    My parents helped me at home.**

My parents watched Landon for me at home so I could do my homework. They also watched him, for free, while I went to work at Five Guys in the evenings. They would put him to bed, and he would be asleep when I got home. Working part time for minimum wage at a burger place didn't exactly provide the most lucrative pay, so if I had to pay for childcare while I worked it would not have been worth my time. In a sense, it really didn't make much sense for me to work, but I think my parents encouraged me to so I could *feel* like I was doing the right thing. My small paychecks paid for most of Landon's diapers, formula, etc., which made me feel like I was providing for him financially.

**4.    My son's father was involved in his life.**

Although we had a rocky relationship at first, I was blessed to have the other parent eager to be involved in my son's life. Even if just for a sleepover for a Friday night (At first it was very hard for me to let go of control) it gave me and my parents a break and my son a relationship with his father. A lot of the teen moms I knew had zero relationship with their child's father- he would either disappear, or if he was still in the picture, he was often abusive. I remember sitting through my pregnancy class and listening to the other mothers vent about their children's' fathers- about burning of Ultrasound DVDs and clothes in the front yard, about constant screaming matches, about physical abuse, or about complete disinterest altogether. By the time Landon was 3, he was spending 50% of his week with his father and 50% with me.

**5.      I received a great education.**

As I described earlier, I was given permission to attend my traditional high school and still access the district's free childcare. The mothers I left behind at the alternative school were not. I may get some hate for writing about this, which is precisely why I have not mentioned the name of the school, but there was no academic rigor in the courses taught there. The pregnancy class was the only one that I found educational and which had a teacher I thoroughly admired (she later came to visit me in the hospital when I had Landon). From the day of their transfer to that school, those moms were immediately facing an uphill battle if they had any desire to pursue a secondary education. They were immediately at a huge disadvantage.

**6.      I earned a scholarship to go to college.**

Before finding out I got the Ford Family Foundation scholarship, I remember discussing with my parents whether college was a realistic possibility for me. Four more years of full-time classes, working in the evenings, and the need to begin paying for a real childcare. The numbers just didn't work out. My parents, although emotionally supportive, could not pay for my school, and could not stay home all day with Landon. I would no longer have the school district's free daycare. The scholarship I received paid for my tuition, my books and supplies, all University fees, my RENT, and my CHILDCARE. Until I saw the first daycare bill, I never realized how significant this was. For 3 days of childcare per week, they paid about $680 per month. They did this for three years of college, until my son was old enough to start kindergarten. So, at $680 per month, for 36 months, they saved me $24,480 in childcare costs. This didn't include the cost of rent: because of the scholarship, I was able to afford a small 2-bedroom apartment. My son, for the first time, had his own bedroom. I remember the day I set up his little mismatched room with secondhand furniture from St. Vincent's and my little brother's old bunk bed from my parents' attic. I sat on the floor and cried in disbelief. I opened my laptop and, sitting there on the floor, I wrote a thank-you email to my scholarship office. Later, when I became a student employee at their office, I found and re-read the email in my file. It was a reminder of how fortunate I felt and how far I had come. No matter where I end up in life, I will always remember the feeling of crying on the floor of Landon's first bedroom.

For years I let my obsession with being different from other teen moms control my life. It controlled who

I hung out with, the things I posted, the way I acted at school, the goals I set. I became so determined to be a good mom that I forgot to be myself. My identity became, to my utter hatred, "teen mom". In my mind, that's who I was. I lived with an unbalanced hatred for being a teen mom and an unwarranted obsession with being a teen mom. I loved it and I hated it- I loved the opportunity to prove myself and beat statistics, but I hated the idea that I might fail at doing so.

Today, I am less hesitant to tell people that I was a teen mom. It often comes up on its own. Just today, one of my new supervisors at work asked me,

"Are you married?" as we walked down the hall.

"No," I said, "but I do have a 7-year-old son." we reached the end of the hallway and she literally stopped in her tracks and turned to stare at me. She stared for at least 5 seconds before asking,

"How old are you?!" the sarcastic Kayla in my head wanted to say something like *'eighteen'* but I told her my age, twenty-three.

"Wow, you were YOUNG when you had your baby! What, like sixteen?!" I awkwardly nodded and made the face I always make, the *yup, yikes, I know* face. I think she felt bad, because she quickly said, "Well that's okay, that's like my mom! She had her first baby at age 16 and had all four of us kids by the time she was 21!" I laughed and said something like *'wow, that's crazy!'* before sitting down at my desk. These interactions don't phase me anymore because they've become so routine- but when I jokingly posted about this particular conversation on my Snapchat, a young pregnant mom I know replied how offensive it was, and told me about similar comments she received when she announced her pregnancy at work. She is twenty-two years old.

It reminded me how differently these kinds of comments and conversations impacted me when I was new to being a young mom- the wound was fresh, and the words cut more deeply. Maybe I've developed a thick skin because I've heard much worse things, or because I now understand how shocking a fifteen-year-old's pregnancy actually is, but I am also aware of how hurtful people's words used to be. To young moms who are currently *in* the midst, it probably feels like they are transitioning from being seen and respected to being looked down upon and belittled. It's like a loss of self. People don't look at you as the same person anymore.

To those moms, if you are reading this, it gets better. It shouldn't have to, I know, people should be kind and respectful and loving and understanding all the time, but they aren't. I don't foresee that changing. But with time, as you adapt to this new version of yourself, as you begin to view yourself as strong and nurturing and grown and independent, people's words won't phase you as much. Sure, they can still hurt, but there comes a point when you are prideful to be who you are, to have grown to fit a new environment, to be strong in a way that your peers can't understand yet. It gets better.

You are beautiful.

You are strong.

You have little eyes watching you and they think you are the most amazing human being in the world. So do I.

## SPLIT IDENTITY

If there is one concept that I had to choose to be the KEY to "Teen Mom Syndrome", it would be the issue of identity. To this day, I'm not sure who I am. I'm a little surer now than I was at fifteen or nineteen, but I honestly still don't know who the real Kayla is.

As the years progressed and my son grew up, he began spending more and more overnights with his father, until we reached a 50/50 parenting schedule. In a short amount of time I went from basing my entire identity on being a mom to having half the week to myself. I didn't know what to do and couldn't quite remember who I was before I became a mom. Of course, I remembered the basics; I was a snarky 15-year-old cheerleader, my life revolved around my friends, and I spent my days designing my Myspace profile and texting my friends. Being suddenly dumped back into freedom as an adult was a shock, because clearly (most of) those things no longer interested me.

It was like I had been in a coma for my teenage years. All I could remember was being fifteen and just *beginning* to experience adolescence, and then being a mother. What had I missed during those 2-3 years that my peers had complete freedom to self-discover? Exactly that, self-discovery. Figuring out my identity. Finding out what I loved and what I hated, what made me happy, who I wanted to be and who I didn't.

In the beginning of my newfound parental freedom, I spent many nights just sitting in my bed, scrolling on my phone. I was so bored; I didn't know what to do. It had been years since I'd been emotionally invested in a TV show or even watched TV. I would close my son's bedroom door when he was away at his dads, so the sight of his empty bedroom didn't sting so much. Over time, I began to develop two versions of myself. One for each half of the week.

During the half of the week that my son wasn't home, I tried my best not to think about him. I know how selfish and horrible it sounds; how could a mother want to forget her own child? It wasn't a matter of forgetting him, it was a matter of trying not to be sad that he was gone. During the half of the week that he was home, I snapped right back into 'Mom Kayla'. I eventually keyed the two terms 'Mom Kayla' and 'Twenties Kayla' and have occasionally used them while trying to explain my life to people.

I know that from the outside, it seems black and white. I am a parent half the week and I have freedom the other half. I have two versions of myself. But I have spent many hours pondering whether any person can truly have two separate identities, or whether they are inevitably tied together. Maybe I bring parts of 'Mom Kayla' into my non-parenting days. I have the desire to control, to nurture, to plan, and I have even found myself exhibiting these habits in my romantic relationships. I've often felt unable to decipher my behavior and figure out why I was doing the things I was doing. I've taken on the role of 'mom' for my significant others because it was the role that came to me most naturally. When I didn't have Landon, I needed someone to 'take care of'. Inevitably, as a teenager/young adult, these qualities can be catastrophic in a romantic relationship.

For years people commended me for 'doing the right thing'. I don't know if they're referring to keeping my baby, finishing high school, going to college, or portraying my life as perfect on social media. This always throws me for a loop because I've never understood how I did anything out of the ordinary. If I'm being completely truthful, which I rarely am, I continued my pregnancy and kept my baby because I had been raised with Christian morals, but also because I *had no other choice.* I've been told that I'm amazing for not having an abortion like other teenagers would have. Again, *I had no other choice.* I'm not saying that I would have had an abortion had I had the opportunity, but I'm saying that it never crossed my mind because I didn't have the opportunity or choice. I was fifteen. I couldn't drive. My parents always monitored my location. They were very religious. Abortion was never an option. I would be lying if I said that the option wouldn't have sounded intriguing when I was fifteen and unable to eat or sleep because I was terrified of my life being over- but I can't say what I would have done because I never had the opportunity to think about that. So why do people give me so much credit when all I've ever done was survive one day at a time?

Adoption wasn't an option either. I wanted to keep my baby and I had my mind absolutely set on that. I reminded my parents relentlessly that I wanted to keep my baby and that, even if I didn't, his father would never let him be put up for adoption. Still, they took the advice of their friends from church and took me to adoption agencies. They forced me to listen to the presentations, they made me talk to the counselors, they made me read the pamphlets. At the time, it made me livid. I was keeping my baby, and that was final. The fact that I couldn't make the decision myself made me feel out of control of my own life. For a long time, I hated them for that. In the end, it was my decision and I prepared to welcome my baby into the world, trading in my teenage years for diaper wipes.

So, can't I now just relive my teenage years now during my non-parenting days? I've asked myself this many times, and I also wonder if other teen mothers have the same feelings I do. I wonder if they feel split between two people, if they feel like they still don't fit in, even in their twenties and thirties and so-on. From my experience, it seemed like all the teen moms fit in with each other except me- so I felt like a misfit. I didn't fit in with my peers, I didn't fit in with the other teen moms, and yet I didn't fit in with any of the older mothers I knew either. I felt alone.

During college, I was even afraid to admit to my classmates that I was a mother. I thought college would be a fresh start for me to feel like I fit in, a breath of fresh air, but it wasn't. It didn't take long for me to realize that I would never have the traditional college experience that my peers did. I would never join a sorority, I would never live in the dorms, and I would never study abroad. Going to a University was a lifestyle for most college students. Their entire life happened on campus. For me, the University was just driving to classes and then going home, back to my reality.

I still deal with this feeling of being torn between two people. I am an artist, so I spend most of my free time painting, but the first half of my week looks drastically different from my second half. If I get invited to a fun night out with friends and don't go, I feel left out. If I do go, I feel guilty. The inner voice I gave myself as a fifteen-year-old still lives in my head, and I still beat myself up for doing anything 'bad'. I feel guilty for drinking, I feel guilty for going to the bars, I feel guilty for being carefree.

If I decide to stay home, I feel 'fear of missing out'. I beat myself up for being antisocial. I tell myself I would have had so much fun if I just made myself go. It's like there is a constant battle in my head between who I should be, but perhaps one version of myself can't exist without the other. I've tried explaining this dichotomy to people, and they are usually empathetic, but I am aware that it's something most people won't understand. If anything, I'm sure I sound like I belong in a mental ward when I talk about the two voices in my head. The thought that maybe other teen moms have had similar experiences is the driving force behind me writing this book.

From my perspective, my confusion regarding my identity isn't completely unwarranted. My son's first day of kindergarten felt like a return to high school. It seemed like all the other parents were in their thirties and on their second or third child. They also all seemed to know each other. I couldn't help but wonder if they thought I was Landon's sister when I showed up to drop him off.

Then one day when I picked Landon up, I heard one of his classmates ask him, "Is that your sister?" he looked at him with confusion and said "No, that's my mom." *Bless his heart,* I remember thinking. *He has no idea how young I look because I'm all he's ever known.* Even today, I wonder if and when he will realize how young I am. It is likely that when he remembers his childhood, he won't remember me as a teenager, he will just remember me as his mother.

His classmate wasn't the only one who noticed my age. Over the years of daycare drop-offs, school plays, and doctors' appointments, the comments have rolled in. "Is that your brother up there?" "You don't look old enough to be a mom, you look 12 years old." "I called your mother and let her know what to bring for Landon, you can ask her."

Landon fractured his wrist last summer and needed a splint. My parents came with me to the appointment, and as the doctor walked in and began explaining the treatment and care for the splint, she locked eyes with my parents the entire time. She didn't glance at me once. It became apparent that she assumed they were Landon's parents, and as soon as she could get a word in, my mother pointed at me and said, "She's actually mom, I'm just grandma." The doctor looked surprised and embarrassed. I was also embarrassed. I left that appointment furious: that was less than a year ago. As much as I may have hoped that being viewed as a teen mom would end once I left my teenage years, it most definitely hasn't. Even now, I find myself purposely not inviting my parents to appointments and events because I want it to be clear that I am my son's mother.

One thing that I have always been determined to do is provide my son with the same life and opportunities as his peers. I never wanted him to realize his parents were different from his friends' parents. I wanted to be just as successful, just as educated, just as polished and just as ADULT as the other parents Landon would interact with during his life. Although well intended, I can now accept that this wasn't realistic.

While in high school, I lived with my parents and my son and I shared a bed and a bedroom. Once I moved out, all I could afford was a small, upstairs apartment off of Main Street. I never invited his friends over to play because I was embarrassed. I was also in college full-time and working, so our place was messy. By the time I got it clean after work and homework and classes, he came home from his dads and it was messy again. Dishes were always piled up and laundry was always overflowing. Of course, I didn't mind it because

I loved every quality moment we got to spend together, just him and I in our own little place. But I kept our home life private and avoided people coming over.

In addition to this, Landon will always be commuting between two homes. Unfortunately, this is only something that we (as co-parents) can try our best to make as convenient and smooth for him as possible. Of course, he asks questions like any seven-year-old does. Sometimes they are age appropriate, and sometimes I tell him that I'll talk to him about it when he's older. In some ways, I will never be able to provide him with the picket white fence life I convinced myself I could at age fifteen. As I've come to accept, my life isn't all picket white fences, and neither is anybody else's life. Life isn't black and white, it's colorful and messy and beautiful all at once. Although he may not have the picture-perfect childhood, I am practicing being less hard on myself for things I will never be able to control.

As I've learned in the process of moving between apartments, duplexes, back home with my parents for brief periods, and back out on my own, the only thing my son really cares about is us being together. More important than the house we live in, the neighborhood our house is in, or whether we have old shag carpet or new vinyl flooring, it matters that I am present.

## SELF-ESTEEM

A struggle that I have a strong feeling is universal to young moms is that with self-esteem. It seems like an inevitable result of skipping one's teenage years and jumping into parenthood. For me, on top of already having a typical teenager identity crisis, I went from being a 110-pound cheerleader to a 165-pound pregnant girl in a matter of months. None of my clothes fit and I looked completely different. My self-esteem plummeted as I realized soon after childbirth that my body would likely never be the same again.

Moms often like to reminisce about their "pre-baby bodies". Well, when I think back to my pre-baby body, I had barely hit puberty. I was fifteen when I got pregnant and I like to believe that my body would have looked very different had I never become pregnant. I had barely begun to form a figure as I began high school, and before I could ever finish puberty, I was pregnant. Truthfully, I wonder often what my body would have looked like once I reached adulthood without ever being pregnant.

For some reason I had a *lot* of weight gain during my pregnancy, which resulted in extreme amounts of stretch marks. My stomach has a permanent line down the center, and as Landon reminded me a few days ago, "your stomach looks like a butt". I know that in his mind he wasn't trying to be hurtful, only observant. However, when most girls my age have never been pregnant and their stomachs are seemingly perfect, it has always been easy to hate my stomach. I haven't necessarily loved the rest of my body either, but my stomach is my least favorite part. Shortly after I gave birth, I would often decline invitations to the lake during the summer because I didn't want to be seen in a swimsuit. Changing in front of other girls gave me anxiety- I was even humiliated around my closest friends. I became obsessed with losing weight, so obsessed that it consumed me.

Towards the end of high school, I had lost all the fifty pounds I gained during my pregnancy. I lived mostly off iced coffees and sparse amounts of food. When I did binge eat, I would take laxatives or force myself to throw up because I was so terrified of gaining the weight back. My relationship with food was very unhealthy and I became obsessed with comparing my image to my peers. I was convinced that I was obese.

Body positivity blogs and family reassured me that my body was beautiful because it created life, it held my son safely until he was ready to enter the world. I knew that they were partially right, but it seemed unfair that I was the only one my age who had to graciously accept such truths. Looks matter to teenagers, and truthfully looks still matter in adulthood. I have struggled with my weight for years since then, but within the last few years I have found the gym to be my therapist.

My self-esteem as a teen mom was linked directly to my friends, to being a mom, and to my dating life. When I felt like I had people, I was content. When I felt rejected or alone, I hated myself. It has been a long journey to become the source of my own happiness.

Because of feeling like an outcast, I developed a desire to please everyone. Everything I did was for everybody else; it wasn't for me. I pushed myself so hard to be the OPPOSITE of a stereotypical teen mom because I wanted to prove myself to my parents and to society. I wanted the kids who made fun of me to feel bad, I wanted my parents to be proud of me, I wanted to say to the world, *"See? You were wrong about me. You underestimated me."* I went to college for this very reason. Once I had crossed that off my checklist, I didn't know where to turn next.

The local news did a piece on my college graduation because I had taken graduation photos with my son that went viral online. The University even shared them on their Twitter page. My son graduated from kindergarten the same year that I graduated from the University, so I ordered him a matching cap and gown online. We posed in front of the University, both toting our matching caps and gowns. I captioned the photos, "You have two options when dealing with the circumstances of your life. 1. Use them as an excuse to fail. 2. Use them as motivation to succeed. We did it baby boy. We're kindergarten and college graduates!" I remember the pride I felt as I posted it- like every late-night doing homework after Landon went to bed had finally paid off, by this one post. This was my *"Ha! Screw you."* to the world.

The news came to my work to interview me and the Foundation's Scholarship Program Director. I spoke about how important the scholarship program was in my success as a nontraditional college student. I watched the piece that night on the news with my family and we were so happy. Feeling like the years of struggling had finally paid off was a major boost to my self-esteem. However, the high inevitably wore off as I realized I now had to find a job and that life moved on past college.

As a cause of my struggle with my self-esteem and identity, I spent many years very depressed. I ignored it until it became concerning and inhibited me from living my daily life, and then I sought professional help. My doctor diagnosed me with depression and prescribed me Sertraline, an antidepressant. My reliance on this medication was something I kept relatively private because I was embarrassed of it. I only released my emotions by painting them and writing them. I did so well at maintaining my image that few people ever realized I wasn't happy.

Although I struggled with depression for years after having my son, it wasn't until I recently did research that I learned that I wasn't an uncommon case. The journal "Pediatrics" did a research study on Canadian women. They found that girls age 15-19 years old experienced Postpartum Depression at DOUBLE the rate of women over the age of 25. Nobody wants to have that discussion though, because of the 'you made your bed, now lay in it' stigma. How can someone complain about circumstances they created for themselves?

It was also determined that teen mothers have higher rates of suicidal ideation than their peers who are not parents. In addition they're more likely to experience Post Traumatic Stress Disorder (or PTSD) because teen moms are also more likely than any other teenager to have experienced mental and/or physical abuse.

Also interesting, while researching I found that according to the Maternal Child Health Journal, teenage mothers have the poorest health index of all categories of women studied. The moms aren't the only ones subject to higher rates of risk: According to the National Institutes of Health, teenage pregnancy has a higher risk of preeclampsia, anemia, premature delivery, and delivering at a low birth weight. According to the U.S. Department of Health and Human Services, kids born to teen mothers face greater challenges, and according to Youth.gov, some effects of having a teenage parent to a child include:

- less prepared to enter kindergarten
- rely more heavily on publicly funded health care
- are more likely to be incarcerated at some time during adolescence
- are more likely to drop out of high school

- are more likely to be unemployed or underemployed as a young adult

So, if teen moms and their children are at such high risks for these issues, why do they have so little support from society? I would argue that the opposite *should* be true. Teen moms should get more support than their older counterparts. Our society should strive to see the success of these young parents and their children. After all, are we not raising up the next generation of our world?

People are so focused on the fact that teen pregnancy *shouldn't happen* that they're unable to see the importance of supporting teenagers that are already moms. See, once the pregnancy happens, *you can't change the past.* Instead of focusing on the events that led up to a teenager becoming a mother, why not put your energy towards focusing on how to support her? I hate to break it to you, but focusing on the past does *nothing.* I'm all for teen pregnancy prevention strategies and sexual education, but once a girl is pregnant and decides to keep her baby, it is not productive to spend time guilting or lecturing her for her actions. I can promise you, she's aware of the consequences without you telling her.

## DATING & RELATIONSHIPS

My self-esteem and my dating life went hand in hand. When I first had my son, dating wasn't on my radar. When you have a baby you don't have time to worry about boys, especially not teenage boys who want nothing to do with a baby. Eventually I dipped my toe in the water as my son grew older and I began to adjust to dating as a mom. I had only ever had one real boyfriend before, and that was my son's father. I quickly learned that sixteen-year-old boys don't want to hang out with babies. However, I had a baby and I wanted to hang out with sixteen-year-old boys. See my problem?

When boys did like me, it never lasted long. I became too familiar with hearing "I like you, but I'm not ready to be a stepdad,", "I can't see myself dating a mom," Or "I'm not looking for anything serious." Often, as soon as I would bring up the subject of my son, I would get ghosted. For those unfamiliar with the term, I mean that these potential boyfriend candidates would disappear completely. Maybe disappearing was easier than telling me the truth: kids scared them.

I don't blame any of them for being uninterested in my life as a teen parent. If you were a sixteen-year-old boy with freedom and friends and an entire future ahead of you with endless opportunities, why on earth would you want to give up having fun to date a girl with a baby? Not to mention, someone else's baby. I often heard,

"I can't date someone and raise some other guys' kid." I wanted to scream, *"I don't want a father for my son! My son HAS a father! I want someone for ME!"* but with years of retrospection, I now know you can't separate the two. Someone for me *must be* someone for Landon too. I spent much wasted effort on boys who required me to separate my life for them—which only added to my identity crisis of being two people. For years, when I hung out with a guy I liked, I completely stopped being a mom. I had to ONLY be Kayla, which was hard. Most high school guys either assumed I was 'easy' because I had a baby and tried to take advantage of that or avoided me altogether.

Dating as a 'Christian girl' was difficult. If you had asked 17-year-old Kayla who her perfect boyfriend would be, she would have said a nice Christian boy who goes to church. The only problem is, once you have a baby at the age of sixteen, you don't exactly feel like the youth group poster child. I was no longer 'pure', I no longer fit into the Christian mold of a pure marriage. I was the impure, broken, used sinner. My dad always reassured me that I would find someone someday, and that the right person would love Landon just as much as he would love me.

With each heartbreak he would piece me back together and tell me that I didn't need to look for love, that maybe I wouldn't find my person until I was older in life, even maybe in my thirties. I hated hearing this. Didn't he know how lonely it was being a mom without a partner? Of course, I wasn't a single mother because my son's father had him half the week, but what term could I use to describe my relationship status and being a mom? A mom who is single? A mother who is alone when she has her parenting days?

When I finally did find myself in a serious relationship, I found a whole new set of struggles. After high school I moved in with my high school boyfriend. Immediately I felt like a mother bird who had to keep her nest full. I quickly realized that, even though we lived together, my partner would never have the same lifestyle as me. He was 18 and he had freedom. He had friends. He liked to go out and have fun, and I don't blame him. What 18-year-old didn't? The animosity grew as my jealousy for his freedom burned inside of me. I began acting like his mother, upset if he wasn't home at a decent hour and I was stuck home alone with my son, while he was having fun that *I couldn't have.*

I told myself I was jealous because I wanted to go out too- but I hated going out. I would rather stay home if I had the option, so I'm not sure why it irked me so badly to see him go out. I selfishly wished he had to stay home like I did. I wished he had the same responsibilities as me, I wished I could make him grow up and that was unfair of me. Just because I grew up so quickly didn't mean I had the right to take away *his* youth. I am thankful for that relationship because it taught me about the darkest and most selfish parts of myself.

So, after that breakup, I was beginning my sophomore year of college, and desperate for a roommate so I could still afford to live in the house we were renting. Now my son and I were back to sharing a bedroom so that my roommate, who I needed to split rent with to afford to stay in the 2-bedroom house, could have the other bedroom. It felt like an immense step backwards.

I quickly learned that college roommates don't want to be parents either. Although they never complained out loud, I felt guilty for every tantrum, every parenting moment, every mess in the kitchen and all the toys all over the place. They had boyfriends over, which of course I was jealous of, because I felt like I deserved that happiness too, and I would never find it. *I'm the one with the kid. I'm the one watching every milestone of his life alone. I deserve happiness. I deserve a family,* I would think to myself. As I had learned within the first year of my son's life, there was something hollow and sad about watching every important milestone in your child's life alone. His first laugh, his first crawl, his first steps, each time I looked over with tears of joy in my eyes and realized I had nobody to share it with.

I dated off and on in college, but nothing ever stuck. I got ahead of myself each time, fantasizing about whether I could have a family with this person. I probably scared some of them off on that premise alone. The main thing I learned about dating in college is that high school boys and college boys aren't very different. They want the same things: to be young and free. One thing nearly none of them want: to be a stepdad.

Relationships after college didn't work out for me either. I soon came to believe that perhaps I was the problem. This feeling of rejection left me with the conclusion that maybe I am the best version of myself when I am alone or maybe I am just not good at dating.

Regardless, over my last five years of adulthood, I found myself jumping from one heartbreak straight to another, leaving myself little to no time to recover in between. I developed unhealthy ways of coping, like drinking or seeking attention from someone new to help me forget about the last person. None of it really helped. The heartbreak just compounded, until I finally reached the catalyst, the final heartbreak I decided I couldn't distract myself from or run away from. I consciously made a decision to break the cycle of unhealthy coping and feel every emotion fully.

I am now on a journey of self-discovery, of healing, of transforming, and of independence. Recognizing my problem was the first step to changing it. I knew I needed to make a change.

Sometimes I wonder, if I had never been a teen mom, would I be seeking out love as much as I have? Maybe feeling like I need a partner to complete me is just part of who I am, or maybe it's a symptom of Teen Mom Syndrome. Looking around at the teen moms who I know, I've noticed from afar that some of them seem to be like me: cycling through relationship after relationship with none of them sticking. Maybe coincidence, maybe not. I've even heard people make comments about some of the young moms in my town. Comments about them 'dating everybody', about them being 'unable to be single', and about them 'looking for a baby daddy'. Although it's easy to laugh along at these comments (and I am ashamedly guilty of doing so), they've never sat well with me because I have done the exact same thing. For some reason, being a mom and being single has felt inevitably wrong to me, like my life is missing a puzzle piece that I desperately needed to find, and *quickly,* before my child grows up.

I have found as I have tried to research what it's like to date for other teen moms that there is relatively nothing written about it. There are articles about dating after a divorce, about *being* a teen mom, about *dating* a mom: but nothing about dating YOUNG men AS a young mom, especially as a teenager. I am sure that I have not been alone in my endeavors to find the 1/1000 guy in their twenties who is willing to take on a parental role for my child. It is unlikely that I am the only teen mom who has a desire to have a family. I know that there are teen moms out there, and I know that statistically not all of them are with their children's fathers.

So, what has it been like for them to date? Am I the only one who has struggled so hard to cope with these issues nobody warned me about? Do other young moms feel that they attract a certain type of person in a partner? Do mothers in their young twenties cycle through failed relationships as much as I have?

## DESIRE FOR A FAMILY

Completely intertwined with my dating life has been my desire to have a family from a young age. This overwhelming urge to create a nest and fill it has caused me to stay far too long in places I didn't belong. It caused me to throw away friendships, to lose sight of my goals, to become obsessive and unhealthy. I wanted so badly to have a family, to *be* a family, that anytime I thought I found the right person, I forgot about all other aspects of my life. I would pour myself into that person, forgetting to fill myself up first.

I would neglect friendships, neglect schoolwork, neglect my artwork, neglect my faith, even neglect my parenting, because I was so focused on securing this idea of having a family with somebody. I daydreamed of fairytale engagements, of Pinterest perfect weddings, of pregnancy announcements and of little feet pattering on the floor, running excitedly to see their daddy after work. This was my dream. It controlled much of my life.

I would be lying if I said it doesn't anymore- I've just decided to stop searching for it.

I put expectations on partners that were probably unrealistic. I wanted them to hurry up and settle down, to make my son and I their priority, to see us as their family. I made stupid mistakes because I believed they would get me one step closer to having the life I wanted. Often, I put my son's heart at risk of being broken because I was so convinced that this time was it- this was the person I would be with forever. I even moved my son in and out of houses/apartments because of it. Not to say that because I was obsessed with settling down, I didn't love my partner- I absolutely did, wholeheartedly. I just also loved the idea of what the *future* version of them could be. Maybe I loved the future version of them more than the version standing in front of me.

When my son turned two, I was eighteen. Right around then, I started *really* wanting another baby. I missed being pregnant, I missed having a newborn, and I didn't want Landon to be an only child. When he began staying more nights with his father, my nest felt even emptier, and the desire to have more kids became stronger. When I had been pregnant, so was my youth pastor's wife. It was even more convenient that she was pregnant only a few months ahead of me. She gave me her maternity clothes as she outgrew them, her baby clothes as her son outgrew them, toys, everything you could think of. We bonded over being pregnant together. I sat by her side at her baby shower as she opened presents and we whisper-joked about being the two pregnant women up front, since nobody knew yet that I was pregnant.

Right about when I turned 18, she announced that she was pregnant again. For some unexplainable reason, I was jealous. Then it was the young mothers I went to the alternative school with. They announced second and third pregnancies and I was jealous. They announced engagements and I was jealous. Life seemed to continue to move on for them, and mine felt stagnant. I wanted nothing more than to have my own family, to experience what a happy and exciting pregnancy felt like, and to do it with a partner instead of with my parents.

Soon, every pregnancy announcement I read on Facebook gave me a little sting in my chest. Announcing my pregnancy had been shameful and looked down upon. Every gender reveal video on Facebook reminded me that I hadn't have one. Every family photo reminded me that I didn't have one of my own. When I was pregnant and felt alone during high school, I remember rubbing my belly and whispering, "just you and me, baby. Just you and me." It felt like I had jinxed myself.

My son's father then got married, and him and his wife soon welcomed a beautiful baby to their family. Finding out that I wouldn't be the one to make my son a big brother for the first time was devastating for me. I didn't know how to put the hurt into words- I felt so selfish. I had to come to accept the fact that I would never witness all of the 'firsts' of him being a brother, that there would be an entire chunk of his identity that I wouldn't know. I had dreamt for years of him someday holding my next baby for the first time, of him helping me pick out baby names, of him growing to love this little human and watching him become protective over them. For a while, it felt like that dream had been taken from me. With time I learned to accept it and feel gratitude for the family life that they were able to give him, even if I couldn't yet. My son loves being a big brother, and I look forward to the day that I get to know that side of him too.

Anytime I tried to express this jealousy and desire to anyone, mostly my parents, they would remind me how fortunate I am to have a little sidekick who loves me with all his heart. I would feel guilty for wanting anything more than my son's love and affection: why couldn't I be happy with just that? Dating left me feeling guilty constantly, guilty for needing to seek any other kind of love than my child's. I never wanted him to feel like he wasn't enough to make me happy.

The desire to have a family paired with the fact that I'm already a mom has put a lot of pressure on me as I have looked for a partner. Even though I always told myself (and them) that I wasn't looking for a role model for my son and there was no pressure to be involved in his life, none of that could be true. Of course, any person I have any chance of a future with has to fit into my son's life somehow. This has eliminated many bad candidates and has reminded me time and time again that the only sources of happiness I should need are myself and my child.

This desire to settle down has felt like a double-edged sword. I have been left facing the question of whether I should leave partners who weren't ready to settle down solely based on that premise- I would be leaving for what exactly, to be alone and even further from the goal of having a family? If I love someone, should I be patient and wait for them to grow up? If I am willing to leave a partner because they don't want to have a family for a long time, will people say I didn't actually love them? Would true love be enough to overcome my heart's desire to have more children and have a full nest?

In my experience, love isn't always enough. You can love someone who is extremely toxic for you, and someone can love you despite *you* being extremely toxic for *them*. You can love someone who wants their life to look completely different than how you want yours to look. You can love someone who is your polar opposite. *That doesn't mean you have to pursue a life together.* For a long time, I have struggled to let go of people, because I was not only letting go of the person, but letting go of the entire future I had planned in my head. The future marriage, the future babies, the future years of happiness and prosperity. I spent more time in the future than in the present and it caused me to stay for too long in places I didn't belong.

## FRIENDSHIPS

I have another confession. I struggle with making and maintaining friendships. For those who really know me, that probably isn't a huge surprise. Although people always tell me that I seem outgoing, I am naturally an introvert. At one time, before becoming a young mother, I was fairly social, but now being around lots of new people drains me. When I was pregnant and returned to my traditional high school, most of my friends (mostly theatre kids that I'd known since elementary school) disassociated with me. They were smart, they took AP classes, they performed in the school theatre, and they were going places in life. A pregnant sophomore in high school doesn't exactly fit into that friend group anymore.

The only friend I could rely on was my childhood best friend. She stuck by my side through everything; through my first failed relationship, through my pregnancy, through my transition to being a mom, through my identity struggles, through every breakup, through every move, for everything. I came to accept the fact that I'd never make another friend like her because nobody would understand me in the way that she did. She knew every version of Kayla that has ever existed, and every phase of my life. If I made myself hang out with someone new, it felt awkward and forced. I didn't want to (or know how to) explain all of these sides of me, all of these facets of my life that my best friend just *knew*. She didn't need any backstory or any explanation, she had been through it all with me.

In college, we were both recently single and became roommates. This chapter of my life was the closest thing I had to a normal college experience. We would bounce between each other's doorways, always bugging each other, always deciding to drive to the Wendy's 20 minutes away at 11 pm, always making plans for the upcoming weekend. She hung out with Landon and I, she helped me discipline him, and she loved him. We even adopted a dog together. It was almost like we were a family.

Shortly into our roommate adventure, my best friend became no longer single. I quickly realized how lonely I was and I became bitter and jealous. I felt like I deserved happiness too. We began to get on each other's nerves in the way that roommates inevitably do and I let my jealousy ruin the friendship. I made stupid decisions out of jealousy, I lied to try to cover them up, and after a large falling out (that was my fault) we stopped talking. And alas as I confessed earlier, I'm not good at making new friends. Wouldn't that time machine I mentioned previously be nice?

Other than my best friend, I made some surface level friendships in high school, mostly with people I had classes with. We didn't hang out outside of school because that's when I had to be a mom. After graduation, I wasn't surprised that none of them stayed in contact. I didn't really make many friends in college either because I was too shy to talk to anyone or speak up in class. I did become friends with one of the other scholarship office work-study students named Rachel and she later became my roommate too. Today, she is one of my closest friends; I was even a bridesmaid in her wedding. As her roommate I experienced a second wind of a taste of normal college experience. We were both responsible, but we both also liked to have fun in our free time. We did normal college kid things on the weekends when I didn't have my son. We even spent hours laying on my bed one night just reading the book of Revelation and discussing the end of the world. Rachel became a friend that challenged me, pushed me, and encouraged me to be a better person.

When I think about why it is so hard for me to make friends, I think about my social anxiety. The last time I felt normal was when I was fifteen. From the age of fifteen I didn't know how to be a normal girl. I didn't know how to relate to normal teenage girls. I still don't know how to relate well to normal 23-year-old girls.

I overthink before I speak, and when I finally do speak, I overthink every word I said. I'm desperate for friends, but when I'm around people I'm desperate to be alone. It takes me a long time to get attached to someone, but once I am attached, I become codependent. I have come to accept that I am happy living a solitary life with a very small circle.

I believe that being a teen parent affects a young mother's ability to relate to her peers, and this affects how she forms friendships. I have witnessed a sort of sisterhood between teen moms I knew from high school- but I also never felt like I fit into it. Maybe, secretly, none of them did either. I guess I'll find out when I publish this book.

## CHASING DREAMS

One thing about becoming a parent is that your priorities instantly change. Your life isn't about you anymore: it's about your child. You wake up every day and you get sh*t done for *them*. It doesn't matter what *you* want anymore. This, along with my scholarship, is one of the reasons I went to college. Society told me it was the right thing to do. The world tells us that if we want to be successful, if we want to make more money, if we want to be better people, we have to go to college right out of high school. Being a teen mom only motivated me more to do the 'right thing' with my life.

So, I didn't plan on chasing my dreams. Can you imagine what people would have said about me as a young mom if I had told everyone I was going to skip college and try to sell paintings for a living? They would say I was irresponsible and a bad mom. Or what if I wanted to move to a big city to try and make a name for myself as an artist? That would be selfish too, uprooting my son's life and taking him farther away from his father. The enthralling part about graduating and becoming an adult (for most 18-year-olds) is the vastness of possibilities for your future. The idea that you can be and do anything you want, that your entire life is a blank canvas ahead of you, is so sensational. You can move to a new place, you can take risks, you can live carelessly and selfishly for the first time. Well, not as a parent.

So, I got a degree I don't use. At first, I wanted to major in Human Physiology with the end goal of going to medical school and being an obstetrician. I wanted to be rich, remember? Then I failed Biology 101 and quickly crossed that career off my list. I took some Family & Human Services classes and liked those, but didn't love them. Art history class seemed like a great idea until I took it and it bored me out of my mind. Every idea I had for a possible future career quickly diminished. Soon, I was entering my junior year at the University, running out of scholarship funding, and still didn't have a major.

I finally decided to just major in Spanish because Spanish was the only subject I really enjoyed and wanted to continue taking. I couldn't realistically study abroad because I couldn't leave Landon for 3 months and I couldn't bring him with me- so I was allowed to fulfill my requirement by working in a high school classroom. I pondered the idea of being a Spanish teacher or a translator. I spent a term as a TA in a Spanish class at my old high school but it just didn't fit me quite right. I graduated with my Bachelor of Art in Spanish, satisfied just to have gotten a degree at all. Then I was thrown into the real world.

After college and my student job at the scholarship office ended, I naively decided to attempt being a full-time artist. Landon and I moved back into my parent's house to save money on rent and I told myself I would paint every day. I don't think I painted once that summer. There wasn't really space for me to get messy with paint in my parents' small house, I had run out of artistic inspiration, and I was miserable living at home again. Broke, bored, and feeling lost, I got a job at a coffee stand.

Then, I read *The Defining Decade: Why Your Twenties Matter and How to Make the Most of Them* by Meg Jay. It was recommended to the scholars at my final leadership conference by multiple keynote speakers, and my scholarship office staff had gifted it to me as my farewell present when I graduated. In *The Defining Decade,* Jay describes her experience as a clinical psychologist with many twenty-something year old clients. The book was incredibly eye opening and I would recommend it to *everyone.* Teenagers, twentysomethings, parents to teenagers, everyone.

When describing one of the twentysomethings she provided therapy for, Jay used the term 'The Starbucks Phase'. She uses the term to describe the common theme of underemployment post-graduation. She points out that finding a sort of temporary, no-skill needed job to bridge the gap until you find your career can in fact hurt your resume. Jay argues that in reality, many twentysomethings are just procrastinating making a career decision, because there is a subconscious fear that taking a step in any direction at all might lead to failure- so they refuse to step at all. They graduate, work at coffee shops, 'find themselves', and waste precious time procrastinating.

When I read it, I felt personally attacked. I had graduated college, had no idea what I wanted to do with my life, had failed at being a full-time artist, and had gotten a minimum wage job at a coffee shop. So, I pulled out my laptop and began applying for jobs online.

A month later I started as an administrative assistant at a private money lending and investment company. It was nothing extravagant by any means, but it was a step. A step towards something, a boost to my confidence, a foot in the door of a professional workplace. Or, as Meg Jay would say, it gave me *identity capital.* If you want to know what that means, read her book. Seriously, do it.

Now, I am still working for the same company and I am an artist too. I have been selling my paintings and digital artwork on canvases, posters, shirts and stickers, on my website and at the local Saturday Market, for three years now. Then a few months ago, while scrolling on Craigslist out of boredom, I found an industrial warehouse space for a good price near my house.

I heard a little whisper in the back of my head. *Do it.* So, I did. I took a calculated risk. I rented out the space and I got to work. After painting the walls, the concrete, the sink and doors, buying tables, chairs, easels, aprons, and paintbrushes, I was ready to host my first Paint & Sip class. My first two sold out, I have three more scheduled, and I'm overwhelmed with requests to travel and do private paint parties at family events and bachelorette parties.

Most people wait until they've reached the successful ending to tell a story, but I don't know if I'll get there yet. I'm still learning in a process of trial and error, but I've decided that chasing my dream of being an artist (but responsibly this time- while still working a regular job) doesn't have to mean I'm a selfish parent.

I include my son in chasing my dreams with me. My favorite part is that he loves art and wants to be an artist too. He's excited to teach my next paint class with me, although we will see if he gets shy when he shows up and sees all of the people. He often paints with me and his teachers always compliment his artwork. He's even auctioned off some of his paintings on eBay and chosen to donate the proceeds to charity.

By choosing to pursue what makes me truly happy, I am setting an example for my son to believe in himself. If he has a dream, I sure as hell am going to encourage him to chase it, because I wasn't really encouraged to chase mine. Being willing to be vulnerable by sharing your passion and creation with the world takes courage. It is, at times, exposing the most intimate parts of yourself to criticism. That's how I feel about this book as I finish the process of writing it- in the beginning I was confident that I wanted to publish it. The closer I get to the end, the more scared I get. Scared of criticism, scared of offending someone, scared of forgetting something important and scared of failure.

But just as I want to teach Landon, you will never make progress by staying stagnant. In order to grow you have to step out of your comfort zone and take risks. Failure is part of the journey to success. So, for now, I will continue to work, and Landon and I will continue to pursue our futures as famous artists. Hey, if I don't make it, maybe he will.

## THE FINALE

As a scholarship office employee, I got to help prepare and host the summer leadership events that I also attended. During the final scholarship leadership conference that I worked, I was introduced to our speaker for the weekend, Kristen Hadeed. Instantly I was drawn to her story. In college, Kristen founded a company called Student Maid. In her keynote speech, along with her TED Talk that you can find online, Kristen narrated her entrepreneurial childhood and what led her to start her own business.

That wasn't the fascinating part. The hook was how many times she confessed to messing up, *big time.* As a college student starting a business and hiring her first employees, she made a *lot* of mistakes, some costing her tens of thousands of dollars, or even causing all of her employees to walk out on her at once.

This is the part of her story that she embraces: she wrote a book called *Permission to Screw Up.* What makes Kristen so inspirational isn't her huge success as

147

a young female CEO, her TED Talk, her massive social media following, or her incredible book. It's how many times she has fallen on her face and gotten back up. That's exactly what her book is about: giving yourself permission to fail. Forgiving yourself. Falling down and getting back up. Learning from your mistakes. Being kind to yourself.

I have made so many mistakes that I can't even remember all of the ones I've made *today*. I have made choices that have had permanent ramifications on my life and on the lives of others. I have hurt others and I have failed as a parent, time and time again. Yet each morning, the sun continues to rise, the birds continue to chirp, and every day is an opportunity to start fresh. In my opinion, that's the best part about life. Sometimes, when you've hit rock bottom, the only thing you can do is take a deep breath and get back up. You can't change your mistakes. You can't fix everything that you've broken. You can, however, choose to learn from your experience and be a better version of you the next day.

Being a mother is hard. Being a teen mother is even harder. There is no manual on how to be a parent, there is no manual on how to be a teenager, and there is no manual on how to be a parent and a teenager simultaneously. I would argue that every teen mom does the best that she can, the best she knows how to do. There are times that we, as humans, fail miserably and humiliatingly. We mess up. We ruin things. We hurt people. We are also capable of evolving.

During many of my hysterical rants, my loved ones have reassured me that I'm no longer a teen mom. They have reminded me that the past is the past and I am a grown woman now, so I should let myself move on. These words are enticing but I've never felt like they are true. As I have always felt in my soul, *teen mom* isn't something I used to be. It is who I am and who I will always be. Since before I had a fully developed frontal cortex, it was intertwined into the deepest fibers of my being that I was two people at once: child and parent. I will always be dancing between the threshold of two

149

realities and two versions of myself, and this is inescapable.

My hope is that as more time passes, it won't have to be a downfall. Rather, it will be a beautiful side of me and a beautiful side of other women like me. A demonstration that I, along with so many other young mothers, can live a multifaceted human experience.

One of my favorite quotes I learned as a Spanish student was by Charlemagne:

"To know a second language is to possess a second soul."

That is how I view my experience as a teen mom; I will always possess two souls.

# NOTES

*About Teen Pregnancy.* (2019, March 01). Retrieved April 22, 2020 from
https://www.cdc.gov/teenpregnancy/about/index.htm


*Screening for Postpartum Depression in Adolescent Mothers.* April 1, 2014. American Academy of Pediatrics. American Academy of Pediatrics


B;, P. (2012, July 16). *Teen Motherhood and Long-Term Health Consequences.* Retrieved June 19, 2020, from https://pubmed.ncbi.nlm.nih.gov/21656056/


Health, O. (2019, May 13). *Teen Pregnancy and Childbearing.* Retrieved June 19, 2020, from https://www.hhs.gov/ash/oah/adolescent-development/reproductive-health-and-teen-pregnancy/teen-pregnancy-and-childbearing/index.html

*Adverse Effects*. (n.d.). Retrieved June 19, 2020, from https://youth.gov/youth-topics/pregnancy-prevention/adverse-effects-teen-pregnancy

Nall, R. (2016, September 19). *Effects of Teenage Pregnancy: Mental Health*. Retrieved June 19, 2020, from https://www.healthline.com/health/pregnancy/teenage-pregnancy-effects

Jay, M. (2016). *The defining decade: What your twenties matter and how to make the most of them now*. Edinburgh, United Kingdom: Canongate Books.

Hadeed, K., & Sinek, S. (2017). *Permission to screw up: How I learned to lead by doing (almost) everything wrong*. NY, NY: Portfolio/Penguin.

Ramsey, D. (n.d.). *Financial Peace University*. Retrieved June 16, 2020, from https://www.financialpeace.com/

Printed in Great Britain
by Amazon